THE JOY OF DANCING

THE
NEXT STEPS

Ballroom, Latin and Jive
for Social Dancers of All Ages

PEGGY SPENCER MBE

CARLTON
BOOKS

ACKNOWLEDGEMENTS

Written & compiled by
PEGGY SPENCER MBE

Consultant editor
ANNA McCORQUODALE

Dance steps photographer
HEINZ LAUTENBACHER

Dance steps performed by:
Ballroom
CHRISTOPHER HAWKINS & HAZEL NEWBERRY
Latin
JOHN BYRNES &
JANE LYTTLETON

Professional dance pictures ©
RON SELF

Dance shoes pictures
DANCESPORT INTERNATIONAL LTD

ADVICE TO THE READER

Before following any exercise advice contained
in this book, it is recommended that you consult
your doctor if you suffer from any health problems
or special conditions, or if you are in any doubt
as to its suitability.

First published in Great Britian in 1999 by
Chameleon Books
an imprint of André Deutsch Ltd

This edition published in 2005 by
Carlton Books
20 Mortimer Street
London W1T 3JW

Printed and bound in Dubai

A catalogue record for this book is available from
the British Library

ISBN 1 84442 413 8

Designed by Anita Ruddell

FOREWORD

As Chairman of the British Dance Council, I am delighted to have been given the opportunity to contribute to this book.

Having tempted the reader's palate with *The Joy of Dancing for Absolute Beginners of all Ages*, Peggy Spencer delves a little deeper with this second book aptly entitled *The Joy of Dancing – The Next Steps*.

Peggy carefully leads the reader along the path to greater proficiency by informing and enriching their understanding of dance and, consequently, she very skilfully draws the reader inexorably to a greater enjoyment of dance. As well as the pleasure dancing provides, there is also a hidden value often not appreciated by those on the outside looking in, this being that many forms of exercise become a chore, endured only to keep fit; dancing, however, is always fun, while at the same time it is a great help in keeping the body trim and healthy. The dictionary defines the word 'dancing' as being use of limbs for health. With dancing, you can confidently add the words 'fun and enjoyment'.

Peggy Spencer has once again in this book passed on her enthusiasm and love of dance, and she gets the message across that dancing is a timeless and constant joy.

The book's clarity and straightforward approach makes it very easy to follow and therefore enables the reader to take the second step on the journey into the wonderful world of dancing.

Read and enjoy this book and I know you will be eagerly awaiting the time when you will be able to take up the *third* step.

Freddie Boultwood
Chairman
British Dance Council

CONTENTS

'HELLO AGAIN' FROM PEGGY SPENCER

CHAIRMAN OF THE IMPERIAL SOCIETY OF TEACHERS OF DANCING

EAR DANCERS

I said in my introduction to my first book *The Joy of Dancing – For Absolute Beginners*, if you can master the basic steps you will always be able to enjoy social dancing on all sorts of occasions. Now in *The Next Steps* you can add to the skills you have already learned.

Once again I have tried to help you as much as possible with photographs and text which are easy to follow and to practise from. I can't stress enough how important it is to practise if you are to get the most out of Ballroom and Latin American dancing.

You will discover that approximately three new steps have been added to the popular dances this time, and each one will enhance your enjoyment and allow you to expand upon your style. With this book, I have included a chart which gives you the correct directions to follow around the dance floor. Do study it and learn the meaning of terms like 'towards wall' and 'towards centre'. All this detail will help you and your partner to enjoy the whole 'moving' experience of social dancing. Remember, ballroom dancing is not a sport that generates bruises and broken bones.

I know you will enjoy learning and dancing *The Next Steps*. Have lots of fun practising and don't
forget that your local dance school can add the finishing touches.

Happy Dancing.

Peggy Spencer

INTRODUCTION:
HOW TO USE THIS BOOK

*T*HIS BOOK HAS been prepared for the social dancer who is trying to add one or two steps to their beginner's programme. It is not wise to have a large programme of figures in every dance. Floors are usually crowded (a large programme is usually for the medallist or the competition dancer who rehearses every day). The social dancer just wants to be able to dance, chat at the same time, enjoy the music and be able to manoeuvre around a small floor.

In this book the dances are divided into two sections. There are the traditional Ballroom dances – the Waltz, Foxtrot, Tango and Quickstep, and then the Latin dances – the Rumba, Samba, Cha Cha Cha and Jive. Any average dance programme will contain one each of the above dances. The repeats are usually the Quickstep, Foxtrot and Waltz. An average programme would have three or four Quicksteps and at least two Waltzes, so it is wise to make sure that they are your most rehearsed dances. The ideal way to work is to study the book, get a feeling for all the steps and then visit a dancing school for the extra help that a professional teacher can give. You will probably need help on directions, leading and timing. Then you may perhaps take up dancing as a hobby and study for medals, adding more to your basic programme.

Remember that dancing at any level will improve your health, help your social life and give you that added dimension of security whenever you are invited to a party or dance, or go on a cruise. Whatever you are hoping to achieve, I would like to emphasize that to get that final polish it is best to go to an experienced dancing teacher who will help you to put all the steps you have learned into the right order, and make them work together well.

HOW TO STUDY AND REHEARSE
Select one dance and study it with the music until you are quite familiar with the name of the step, the basic action, the direction you need to move around the room, and how to lead or follow and hold your partner. Work on one dance at a time because each dance has its own character and feeling, so it is wise to make yourself familiar with it until you are as efficient as possible. Always step out the foot positions first until the steps become very familiar and easy. Then study the next aspect – where is your partner? Where are your arms? What is the rhythm? How should you stand? Gradually add these essential ingredients to the steps and remember that your coordination is of major importance. Commencing and finishing positions of the figure are very important, your wall-to-wall guide (see page 10) will help you to understand when a figure commences towards the outside wall or towards the centre. Think of your room as a circle and travel anticlockwise around it. Remember that not all figures face the direction of the circle; some commence facing towards the outside wall or towards the centre.

Dancing can make you feel happy, because moving to music is a most enjoyable pastime. Dancing helps to establish new friendships and it helps to create an atmosphere of happiness.

WHAT TO WEAR

$\mathscr{T}$HE CORRECT CLOTHES for dancing depend on the type of function you are attending. In general the golden rule is to wear clothes that are comfortable, smart and suitable for dancing. The exception is a holiday disco, where the clothes and shoes are usually casual. Whether it is a dinner dance, party or a holiday dance, a few general rules will cover everything.

Ladies should try to avoid wearing fluffy tops that might cover your partner in fluff, or wearing dresses with big hanging sleeves, as this makes it difficult for your partner to put his right hand around you. If you are wearing a long evening dress, always look in the mirror and check that when you step backwards you are not going to step onto the skirt of your dress, which may either tear the dress or result in a fall.

Men should always check to see if a dinner jacket or suit is required. Many clubs do not allow a man in without a tie.

SHOES

The correct footwear is essential to any dancer. You don't have to have top-of-the range shoes, but your shoes should be comfortable, flexible and suitable for dancing.

'Trainers' are not recommended for any form of Ballroom or Latin dances except perhaps for the Rock or Jive, or casual dancing on the beach.

All dance shoes should fit perfectly, and not be too new or slippery. Wear new shoes in around the house first.

Ladies should avoid slingbacks. They can be extremely dangerous as well as uncomfortable, as they do not give you enough support when stepping backwards. Heels that are too high should also be avoided.

The shoes shown are a selection recommended for Social dancers by DanceSport International from their new collection.

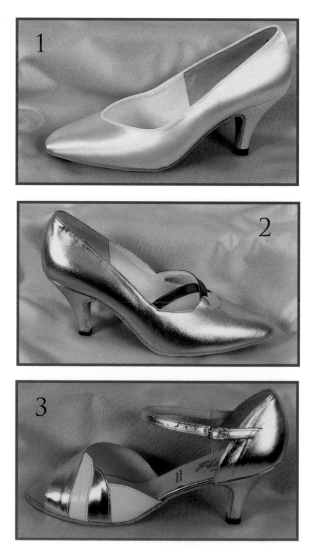

1 *Ballroom: Lady's white satin court shoe. The great advantage of this simple shoe is that it is both elegant and comfortable. It can also be dyed to match your dress.*

2 *A two-tone leather court shoe with crossover straps which create a fashion detail. The medium high heel helps to give balance. Too high a heel will be difficult to dance in and may also upset your balance.*

3 *Latin: Lady's leather two-tone Latin dance shoe. These shoes are open at the end to allow the toes to spread. This is required in the Latin dances as much of the footwork is on the ball of the foot.*

4 *Ballroom: Man's shoe. This can be either in leather or patent leather. It should be comfortable and fit perfectly with approximately a one inch heel.*

5 *Latin: Man's leather shoe. This shoe is made of very soft leather or nubuck. The softness allows for the total flexibility of the feet and toes. A Latin dancing shoe should fit like a glove. The heel is higher than a ballroom shoe – about one and a half inches.*

MUSIC

Music is the very essence of dancing and it is therefore very important when learning your new steps to study them with the right music. One of the first rules is to choose music that is the correct tempo for the dances you are going to do. Remember that not all record shops stock music that is in the required tempo. With the tremendous selection of recordings available it is possible to obtain almost any good dance music in all sorts of tempos from dance specialists (see page 128). Once you have become proficient, you will be able to improvise to almost any music.

Listen to your chosen music, study it, and fit your steps to it. Learn the number of beats and the rhythm of the dances, and then the steps will fit in more easily.

Many functions do not have a Master of Ceremonies and DJs often do not announce dances so you will be expected to be able to recognize a Waltz, Cha Cha Cha or a Rock 'n' Roll piece of music, and know what steps to use.

Each dance has its own character, it's own history and it's own music. By listening carefully and understanding the difference between various dances you will recognize which dance to perform to which piece of music. It is fun to learn as it gives you an insight into how the character of the dance has evolved over the years. Learning about the history and the music of a dance is as essential as obtaining the correct foot positions.

UNDERSTANDING YOUR DIRECTION
AROUND THE BALLROOM

A a social dancer, it is as important to understand your direction around the room when you dance as it is to understand the need to drive a car on the correct side of the road. In the moving dances such as the Foxtrot, the Waltz, the Quickstep and the Samba the direction round the room is anti-clockwise. Imagine bollards down the centre of the ballroom and dance anti-clockwise around them. While you are travelling in an anti-clockwise direction around the room, some of the figures will face towards the centre, then towards the wall, and then towards the line of direction. This is your alignment. Study this chart carefully and understand the meaning of towards the wall, towards centre or line of dance around the room. It is important that you do not encroach on the space of your partner when you dance. Stand upright at all times and don't lean into your partners' top. It is so easy for the man to pull the top of the Lady towards him with his right hand, or for the Lady to pull the top of the man towards her with her left hand. This will put the partnership out of balance and dancing will become very cumbersome and even out of control over a period of time.

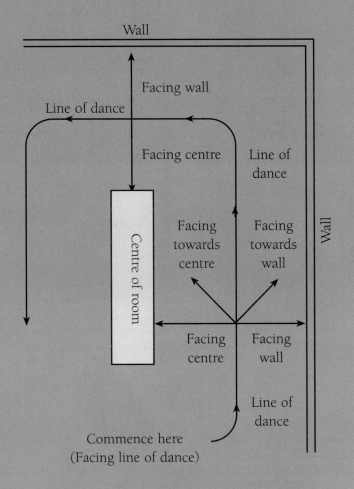

The diagram above shows your journey around the ballroom floor. Note that 'facing wall' and 'facing towards wall' are slightly different directions, as are 'facing centre' and 'facing towards centre'.

WARM-UP TIPS

These tips are directed towards social dancers. Any physical activity requires the body to be ready and taking a few minutes to warm-up will produce rewarding results. The following are a few warm-up tips. Make sure that every action is gentle and performed with care.

Neck Release
Stretch your neck gently upwards to release tension and then turn your head slowly to the right and then to the left. While doing this try to feel tall. This action will help you to achieve good poise.

Shoulders
Roll each shoulder in a half-circular motion and then lift both shoulders up and down to achieve a total relaxed feeling. Relaxed and dropped shoulders are essential for good dancing.

Hips
Hold onto a chair or wall for balance and then free the hip joints by gently swinging each leg forward and back – keeping the foot slightly off the floor. Dancing requires the hip joints to move softly and freely.

Knees
Loosen knee joints by lifting each knee in turn. This will help the fluid to circulate around the knee joints ready for dancing.

Ankles
Extend your foot slightly and circle the ankle, first to the right and then to the left, working on each ankle alternately.

Toes
Dancing requires light movements with the feet. Rise onto your toes and gently lower your weight into the whole of your foot. This is an important exercise. It gives the whole foot a chance to work from the heel to the ball of the foot to the toes, and then from the toes to the ball of the foot to the whole foot.

Hands and Wrists
Extend your arms and circle your wrists. Stretch your fingers, separating each one, and open and close the hands. This is an essential exercise for those who work on computers, to ensure the arms, wrists and hands are relieved of the day's working tensions.

A short set exercise routine each day will help to keep the body, muscles and blood ready for dancing and will also help to relieve tensions. The order in which you do the exercises is up to you. A good idea is to start at the top of the body – neck, shoulders, hips, knees, ankles, feet and toes – or start at the bottom – toes to neck.

These very gentle exercises are not intended to be a full work-out routine. Completing the exercise routine will also help you to understand both balance and continuity of movement.

Walks forward
Start with your weight on your right foot. Walk forward onto your left foot, then walk forward onto your right foot, carefully 'brushing' your right foot past your left foot. Repeat for up to six walks forward.

Walks backwards
Start with your weight on your right foot. Place your left foot back, taking a small step. Extend your foot slightly beyond the body in order not to drop your weight backwards and lose your poise. Repeat this action for up to six walks backwards.

THE WALTZ

HE WALTZ IS A FAVOURITE. Generally the figures are quite easy. Perhaps the most difficult figure in the Waltz is a Spin Turn. Here the important thing is to make sure the lead is given by the male partner. The Waltz can be used as an opening to a dance or as the Last Waltz. It is often used as an anniversary dance or at a wedding.

The history of the Waltz is very interesting and worth an in-depth study. It was one of the first 'together' dances to come to this country

and therefore had a stormy passage, but it has been readily accepted as part of any dance programme. In the case of competition or exhibition dancers it is always included in their programme to enable them to use sentimental music.

Study the photographs and match the positions of the feet with the words. *The Next Steps* are not as simple as the elementary steps, although every figure is based on the basic movement of forward, side, close or back, to the side, close. Every movement is based on those steps. Although the feet may cross behind, as in the Whisk, that is just an alteration in one step. Instead of closing the foot, it is crossing behind, and so on.

The Whisk is a lovely figure to dance and it comes from a moment in history. A dancer was about to close the feet on the basic movement, practising a Waltz, when he decided to cross the foot behind. And so the Whisk or Cross Behind was born. It is perhaps one of the most popular actions in all dances.

When dancing the Whisk or the Cross Behind, take care when you have completed the foot behind, that the Man's toes are facing in the same direction and also that the Lady's toes are facing in the same direction. The next step is forward and the foot needs to be in the correct position: ready to go forward. If the crossing foot is not on the same alignment it will cause you to lose balance and be uncomfortable. Lower the heel gently to the floor: just place and lower it carefully, almost like handling a piece of valuable china.

LEFT TURN

STARTING POSITION

Commence facing partner in normal position facing towards centre, Man's weight on right foot, Lady's weight on left foot.

STEP 1 *Count: 1 beat*
Man: Left foot forward and commence to turn to the left, leading Lady to step back onto her right foot.
Lady: Right foot back.

STEP 2 *Count: 1 beat*
Man: Right foot to side and continue to turn left, leading Lady to step to the side onto her left foot.
Lady: Left foot to the side.

STEP 3 *Count: 1 beat*
Man: Left foot closes to the right foot, leading Lady to close her right foot to her left foot.
Lady: Right foot closes to left foot.

STEP 5 *Count: 1 beat*
Man: Left foot to the side and continue to turn to the left, leading Lady to step to the side onto her right foot.
Lady: Right foot to the side.

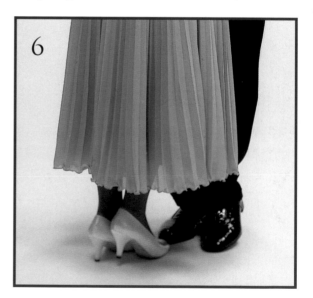

STEP 4 *Count: 1 beat*
Man: Right foot back and continue to turn to the left, leading Lady to step forward onto her left foot.
Lady: Left foot forward.

STEP 6 *Count: 1 beat*
Man: Right foot closes to the left foot, completing the turn to the left and to end facing the outside of the room, leading Lady to close her left foot to her right foot.
Lady: Left foot closes to right foot, completing the turn to the left.

WHISK

STARTING POSITION
Commence facing towards the wall, Man's weight
on right foot, Lady's weight on left foot.

STEP 1 *Count: 1 beat*
Man: Left foot forward, leading Lady to step back onto her right foot.
Lady: Right foot back.

STEP 2 *Count: 1 beat*
Man: Right foot to the side and slightly forward, leading Lady to step back and to the side onto her left foot and preparing to turn her for 'Whisk' position.
Lady: Left foot back and slightly to the side, preparing for 'Whisk' turn.

STEP 3 *Count: 1 beat*
Man: Left foot crosses behind the right foot, leading Lady to turn slightly and cross her right foot behind her left foot.
Lady: Right foot crosses behind left foot, turning slightly to a promenade 'Whisk' position.

STEP 4 *Count: 1 beat*
Man: Right foot forward in promenade position, leading Lady to step forward onto her left foot.
Lady: Left foot forward in promenade position.

STEP 5 *Count: 1 beat*
Man: Left foot to the side, leading Lady to step to the side onto her right foot and returning to normal position.
Lady: Right foot to the side, turning to face partner in normal position.

STEP 6 *Count: 1 beat*
Man: Left foot closes to the right foot, leading Lady to close her right foot to her left foot and ending in normal position.
Lady: Right foot closes to left foot to end facing partner in normal position.

RIGHT SPIN TURN

STARTING POSITION

Commence facing towards wall, Man's weight
on left foot, Lady's weight on right foot.

STEP 1 *Count: 1 beat*

Man: Right foot forward, leading Lady to step back onto her left foot and commence a turn to the right.

Lady: Left foot back commencing to turn to the right.

STEP 2 *Count: 1 beat*

Man: Left foot to the side, continue to turn to the right, leading Lady to step to the side onto her right foot.

Lady: Right foot to the side.

STEP 3 *Count: 1 beat*

Man: Right foot closes to the left foot, completing the first part of the turn, leading Lady to close her left foot to her right foot.

Lady: Left foot closes to right foot.

STEP 4 *Count: 1 beat*
Man: Left foot back- (small step) and spin half turn to right on left foot, leading Lady forward onto her right foot and to spin to her right.
Lady: Right foot forward and spin to the right, Lady's right foot will be placed between partner's feet.

STEP 5 *Count: 1 beat*
Man: Right foot forward continuing to spin to the right ending between partners feet.
Lady: Left foot to the side and very slightly back. (Spin Action).

STEP 6 *Count: 1 beat*
Man: Left foot to side and very slightly back, completing the turn to the right and leading Lady forward on the right foot to end between partner's feet.
Lady: Right foot placed forward between partner's feet.

STEP 7

Count: 1 beat

Man: Right foot back, leading Lady forward onto her left foot, with a slight turn to the left.

Lady: Left foot forward with spin turn.

STEP 8

Count: 1 beat

Man: Left foot to the side, continue to turn to the left, leading Lady to the side onto her right foot.

Lady: Right foot to side.

STEP 9

Count: 1 beat

Man: Right foot closes to left foot, completing slight turn to the left, leading Lady to close her left foot to her right foot.

Lady: Left foot closes to right foot.

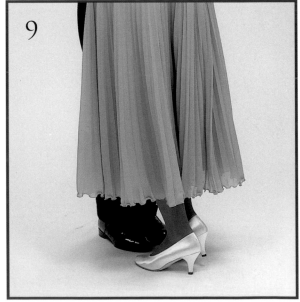

SPECIAL TIPS

★ Use a walking step on all forward leads. The foot should be used as you would to walk to the bus stop, with a heel lead. Try to use beats two and three on the ball of the foot, so in each bar of the music beat one will be a strong step and beats two and three will be lighter steps. Wear comfortable shoes and ensure they are not slippery. There are special non-skid shoes which are designed for dancing, to give the feeling of security in the foot.

★ The Hold

As the dance is in close hold try not to pull the Lady forward towards the partner or equally, try not, as the Lady, to use the left hand to pull the Man towards you. Both should stand upright on their own feet and dance throughout in their own space, not at any time invading each other's space.

★ Suggested Choreography

Right foot basic, left foot basic
Right foot basic, left foot basic
Right turn
Right foot basic, left foot basic
Right foot basic
Left turn
Whisk and right foot basic
Left foot basic, right foot basic
Left foot basic
Right turn and spin
Left foot basic and then select any of the figures to start again.
This is only a suggested way of putting the figures together. It is not essential to follow this pattern. The dancer should be able to improvise according to the space available.

★ Spin Turn

The spin turn is quite difficult to do and needs lots of practice to get the poise and balance right. ▷

★ The Arms

For the Social dance, although the arms are not held wide, they can become very heavy, particularly the top part of the Lady's arm. Be very conscious that the arms are held lightly and exercise in order to be able to do this consistently throughout a dance.

★ The Whisk

The Man's lead is very important. He should lead the Lady to turn slightly into the Whisk, but not turn himself. If he turns, the effect is of an open book with both sides open at an equal distance. This will then be difficult to close up again in the following step. So imagine the Man opens the Lady very slightly into the Whisk or Cross Behind position but does not open himself very much at all. ▷

THE MAMBO

THE MAMBO is from the same family of dances as the Cha Cha Cha and Rumba. Here, the step pattern is almost identical to that of the Rumba, but the music is very much faster and therefore the steps are smaller. The hip action is less pronounced and the speed restricts the number of figures that it is necessary to dance. To enjoy the Mambo, the dancer only needs quite a small repertoire of figures, as the art lies in the speed and the feeling of turning to the left, and the rhythm in the use of the feet, ankles and legs. Practise the basic movement forward and back in place, without a turn, until the feet can achieve the speed of the music. The ideal way to practise is to begin slowly at first, and then build up the speed and finally fit it to the music. Having learned the basic steps and achieved the speed, then these next steps will be very entertaining and interesting to add to the choreography.

Mambo music is in four four time, and with three steps to the four beats. The division is step one quick, step two quick and the third step takes two beats and makes a slow. So the timing will be quick, quick, slow – quick, quick, slow. Different parts of the world interpret this music in various ways, so the individual dancer can decide whether the first step is on the first, second or in some cases even on the third beat of the bar. Therefore it is wise to listen very carefully to the music and see which beat comes naturally to you.

The footwork is ball flat throughout, although sometimes the backward step is taken on the ball of the foot only in order not to lose the weight backwards. In addition to this, the small steps of the Mambo make it necessary to have pliable shoes that almost fit the feet like a glove in order to obtain the speed required for this very fast dance.

The entire body should be tall and erect, the weight central, and the head held over the backbone, making sure that neither partner throws the head and chest forward towards each other.

TURNING BASIC WITH CROSS BODY LEAD

STEP 1

Count: 1 beat – quick

Man: Left foot forward and commence to turn to left, leading Lady to step back onto her right foot.

Lady: Right foot back, commence to turn to left.

STARTING POSITION

Commence facing the wall with Man's weight on right foot, Lady's weight on left foot.

STEP 2

Count: 1 beat – quick

Man: Replace weight back into right foot and continue to turn to the left, leading Lady to replace weight into her left foot in place.

Lady: Replace weight forward into left foot.

STEP 3

Count: 2 beats – slow

Man: Left foot to the side in Promenade position, leading Lady to step forward and to the side onto her right foot to end in Promenade position.

Lady: Right foot forward and to the side to end in Promenade position.

STEP 5

Count: 1 beat – quick

Man: Replace weight forward into left foot, in place, leading Lady forward onto her right foot.

Lady: Right foot forward.

STEP 4

Count: 1 beat – quick

Man: Right foot back, leading Lady in front and towards left side, on her left foot.

Lady: Left foot forward, across and in front of man towards his left side.

STEP 6

Count: 2 beats – slow

Man: Right foot to the side, very small step, leading Lady to the side on her left foot to end facing partner in normal position.

Lady: Left foot to the side to end facing partner in normal position.

BACK BREAKER

STEP 1

Count: 1 beat – quick

Man: Left foot crosses behind right foot, leading Lady to cross her right foot behind her left foot. Release left hand from Lady's waist, keep firm hold with right hand on waist. *No* turn for the Man.

Lady: Right foot crosses behind left foot, leaning back slightly from waist, supported by man's right hand/arm with a slight turn to the right.

STEP 2

Count: 1 beat – quick

Man: Replace weight into right foot, in place. No turn, leading Lady to replace weight into left foot.

Lady: Replace weight into left foot with a slight turn to the left.

STARTING POSITION

Commence facing partner with Man's weight on right foot and both hands on Lady's waist, Lady with weight on left foot.

STEP 3

Count: 2 beats – slow

Man: Left foot to the side, leading Lady to step to the side onto her right foot, returning to waist hold. Both hands on Lady's waist.

Lady: Right foot to the side.

STEP 5

Count: 1 beat – quick

Man: Replace weight into left foot, leading Lady to replace weight into her right foot.

Lady: Replace weight into right foot. Commence turn to the right.

STEP 4

Count: 1 beat – quick

Man: Right foot crosses behind left foot, leading Lady to cross her left foot behind her right foot. Release right hand from Lady's waist and keep a firm hold with left hand on waist. No turn for the Man.

Lady: Left foot crosses behind right foot leaning back slightly from waist – supported by man's left hand/arm with a slight turn to the left.

STEP 6

Count: 2 beats – slow

Man: Right foot to the side, leading Lady to step to the side onto her left foot, returning to normal position. No turn.

Lady: Left foot to the side, returning to normal position.

MAMBO CUDDLE

STARTING POSITION
Commence facing your partner in normal position, with Man's weight on right foot, Lady with weight on left foot.

STEP 1
Count: 1 beat – quick
Man: Left foot forward, leading Lady to step back onto her right foot.
Lady: Right foot back.

STEP 2

Count: 1 beat – quick

Man: Replace weight into right foot, leading Lady to replace weight into her left foot and commence turn to her left.

Lady: Replace weight into left foot and commence turn to the left.

STEP 3

Count: 2 beats – slow

Man: Left foot to side almost closing to the right foot, leading Lady forward turning her to her left to end on the Man's right side in a Side-by-Side position.

Lady: Right foot forward and to the side, to Man's right side to end in a Side-by-Side position, having made a half turn to the left.

STEP 4

Count: 1 beat – quick

Man: Right foot forward, leading Lady to step back onto her left foot to end on the Man's right side.

Lady: Left foot back.

STEP 5
Count: 1 beat – quick
Man: Replace weight into left foot, leading Lady to replace weight into her right foot and commence to move in front of the Man.
Lady: Replace weight into right foot moving in front of the Man.

STEP 6
Count: 2 beats – slow
Man: Right foot to the side, leading Lady to step to the side onto her left foot.
Lady: Left foot to the side moving in front of the Man to end on his left side.

STEP 7
Count: 1 beat – quick
Man: Left foot forward, leading Lady back onto her right foot to end on the Man's left side.
Lady: Right foot back on Man's left side.

STEP 8

Count: 1 beat – quick

Man: Replace weight into right foot, leading Lady to replace weight into her left foot and commence to move in front of the Man.

Lady: Replace weight into left foot and commence to move in front of Man.

STEP 9

Count: 2 beats – slow

Man: Left foot step to the side, Lady now in front of the Man.

Lady: Right foot step to the side, passing in front of the Man.

STEP 10

Count: 1 beat – quick

Man: Right foot forward, leading Lady back onto her left foot to end on Man's right side.

Lady: Left foot back to end on Man's right side.

The Man will lead the Lady to change from his right side to his left with slight pressure from his right hand.

STEP 11

Count: 1 beat – quick

Man: Replace weight into left foot, leading Lady to replace weight into her right foot and to commence turn to the left.

Lady: Replace weight into right foot and commence turn to the left to end in normal position.

STEP 12

Count: 2 beats – slow

Man: Right foot almost closes to left foot, leading Lady to face partner in normal position.

Lady: Left foot to the side, completing a half turn – turning strongly – to the left to end facing partner in normal position.

SPECIAL TIPS

The Mambo is a Latin dance and it is a set of basic steps. Once these have been learnt the dance is easy to improvise.

★ The Cuddle

This is as it sounds, with the Man's right hand gently around the lady's waist. He can then gently pull her towards him to form another closed cuddle. ▷

★ Left Hand Hold

Do not hold the hand too tightly: make sure the Man's palm is held upwards and the Lady's palm is held downwards. △

★ The Back Breaker

This is another variation but requires firm support from the Man as the Lady leans backwards. △

★ Promenade Step

Both dancers face forward in a Promenade position. ▷

THE FOXTROT

HERE ARE THREE TYPES OF FOXTROT – the social Foxtrot as in *The Joy of Dancing – For Absolute Beginners*, the Beginner's slow Foxtrot as in this book, and the Slow Foxtrot, as danced by competition and exhibition dancers for very advanced work. The Slow Foxtrot is considered the connoisseur's dance and the famous dancer Len Scrivener always said, 'The first seventeen years are the worst'. This highlights the fact that this is a dance that looks so easy, but the easier it looks, the harder it is to do. The version of the Foxtrot given here introduces the dancer to the action of

passing the feet, which is characteristic of the Foxtrot. In many other dances the feet close, either in the Chassé action, or at the end of a bar of music, but in the Slow Foxtrot the feet are passing most of the way and seldom do they actually close. Because of the consistent rhythm – slow, taking two beats and two quicks – the dance has a feeling of walks on the slow counts, and then soft running steps on the balls of the feet on the two quicks. So you could rehearse the dance in a little sing-song of, 'Walk, run, run – walk, run, run', and this would give the action of the slow, quick, quick and also introduce you to the characteristic already explained of passing the feet and not closing the feet.

Step 1 is taken in line with the partner, which is the walking step, and steps 2 and 3 are taken outside the partner, which is the running effect. Step 4 is in front of partner; steps 5 and 6 are the Lady's steps running outside. Step 7 is in line with your partner and steps 8 and 9 are outside of your partner, with the running effect. The little variation called the Whisk or the Cross Behind gives a change of direction and sets the dancer ready to start the sequence all over again.

The amalgamation here has twelve steps and it can be an advantage, while practising, to count out twelve foot positions.

Because there are so many lovely melodies in Foxtrot rhythm to dance to, this gives the dance an added attraction. Once you have mastered this version of the Slow Foxtrot, it will be easier to go on to the next level.

SLOW FOXTROT (BEGINNERS)

STARTING POSITION

Commence facing towards centre, weight on left foot, Lady's weight on her right foot.

STEP 1

Count: 2 beats – slow
Man: Right foot forward, leading Lady to step back onto her left foot.
Lady: Left foot back.

STEP 2

Count: 1 beat – quick
Man: Left foot forward on toe, moving towards partners' right side, leading Lady to step back onto her right foot.
Lady: Right foot back.

STEP 3

Count: 1 beat – quick
Man: Right foot forward on toe, outside partner, on her right side. Small step leading Lady to step back onto her left foot.
Lady: Left foot back.

LEFT TURN

STEP 4

Count: 2 beats – slow

Man: Left foot forward, commence to turn left, leading Lady to step back onto her right foot.

Lady: Right foot back, commence to turn left.

STEP 5

Count: 1 beat – quick

Man: Right foot to side and very slightly back, leading the Lady to step forward onto her left foot outside partner on right side.

Lady: Left foot forward and slightly to side, outside partner on his right side.

STEP 6

Count: 1 beat – quick

Man: Left foot back, no turn, leading Lady to step forward onto her right foot outside partner on his right side.

Lady: Right foot forward, no turn, outside partner.

STEP 7

Count: 2 beats – slow

Man: Right foot back, leading Lady to step forward onto her left foot *in line* with partner.

Lady: Left foot forward in line with Man.

STEP 8

Count: 1 beat – quick

Man: Left foot to side and slightly forward, turning to face towards the outside of the room, leading Lady to step to the side onto her right foot in front of partner.

Lady: Right foot to the side to end backing outside of room, now in front of partner.

STEP 9

Count: 1 beat – quick

Man: Right foot forward on toe, outside partner on her right side, moving towards outside wall, leading the Lady to step back onto her left foot.

Lady: Left foot back, with partner on outside on right side.

WHISK/CROSS BEHIND

STEP 10 *Count: 2 beats – slow*
Man: Left foot forward, leading Lady to step back onto her right foot.
Lady: Right foot back.

STEP 11

Count: 1 beat – quick
Man: Right foot forward, slightly to the side, turning to face the centre of the room, leading Lady to step back and to the side onto her left foot and preparing her for the Promenade.
Lady: Left foot back and to the side turning to face towards centre of the room, preparing for the Promenade position (Whisk).

STEP 12 *Count: 1 beat – quick*

Man: Left foot crosses behind right foot in Whisk position, leading Lady to cross her right foot behind her left foot.

Lady: Right foot crosses behind the left foot in Whisk position.

STEP 13

Count: 2 beats – slow

Man: Right foot forward in Promenade position.

Lady: Left foot forward in Promenade position.

STEP 14

Count: 1 beat – quick

Man: Left foot forward, leading Lady to step back onto her right foot, turning the Lady to face her partner.

Lady: Right foot back turning to face partner.

Continue into **STEP 3** and repeat the complete sequence of steps as many times as required.

SPECIAL TIPS

★ The Lead

The lead into the Whisk is very important with the Man using his right hand to gently turn the Lady to face the same direction as himself. ▷

★ The Whisk

The Whisk, or Cross Behind is in effect a change of direction. When dancing this basic foot pattern, the dancer is moving towards the outside wall and needs to change direction, so the Man leads into the Whisk or Cross Behind and turns from facing the outside wall to facing towards the centre, which has introduced the change of direction. When completing the Whisk or Cross Behind, and continuing to the next figure, his direction is then moving towards centre. He completes the nine steps which bring him again going towards the outside wall and goes into the Whisk or Cross Behind, which changes his direction again. This little sequence can be repeated round and round the room. △

★ Lady outside on Step 3 of left turn. △

THE SAMBA

THE SAMBA'S exciting, rhythmic music is part of Brazilian culture. It has a tradition reaching back hundreds of years, with many other dances created from this original carnival music. The analysis of each step and timing are very important in order to understand the difference between two steps to a bar of music and three steps to a bar of music, and to distinguish between different actions.

The music is fairly fast and the steps are very, very small, with the action of the knees being of major importance. In fact, it helps tremendously if you exercise the bounce action of the knees independently from working the steps. Listen to the music and bounce your knees up and down to get the feeling of the music through your legs and knees before dancing the steps. This will help to make the dance more free and rhythmically acceptable.

Originally, the Samba had many hand movements because it was danced 'solo' as a Carnival dance. Then it became groomed for the ballroom, to be danced by couples. The social Samba relies on a few steps. These are usually natural opposites and the couple stand just a little apart so that they have got room to do their individual steps. Today there are very few hand movements, except perhaps in an exhibition or competitive Samba. In this advanced form of Samba, a routine can be very cleverly choreographed to contain lots of step patterns, spins, solo work or together work. Steps are very often taken from other dances and introduced into Samba character, producing a very interesting fast-moving and enter-

taining routine. As a social dancer, it is better to have five or six step patterns, to make the choreography suitable for crowded rooms and to enable the dancer to dance and enjoy this delightful music and also enjoy dancing with a partner, without having to remember a long routine.

The music, written in two-four time, has two beats to a bar, usually counted one-two one-two. Movements, like the Whisk, and the Samba Walk, are counted 'one-a-two, one-a-two', the 'a' denotes a ¼ of a beat, so that the division would be ¾ of a beat into the first step, a ¼ of a beat into the second step, and a whole beat into the third step. The hold is loose, with a very small distance between the couple – enough room for the Lady to turn under the arm, if required. The tempo should be about fifty bars per minute. Some orchestras will play it faster, in which case the dancers have to accommodate this.

All steps are taken with the ball of the foot flat, except for the quarter beat steps, which are usually taken on the ball of the foot only. The term 'part weight' used in the description denotes that weight is taken only momentarily on the foot. The flexing and straightening of the knees is of major importance. In the basic bounce with two steps to a bar counted, one-two, one-two, the knees are flexed when the weight is taken onto the stepping foot. In the alternative basic bounce where you have three steps to a bar of music the knees are also flexed when the weight is taken on to the stepping foot. The best thing to do is not to analyse this

too closely but to feel the bounce action when dancing the exercise to the music, and then applying the steps to this. Then the knee action should come naturally.

The Samba, in its social form, travels anti-clockwise around the room. Many figures are fairly static, but the promenade walk would travel anti-clockwise. *Reverse* movements mean turning to the left, *natural movements* mean turning to the right. Figures like the whisk and the ladies underarm turn are danced on the spot.

Shoes should be flexible with soft soles so that the foot can flex, contract and straighten with the knee action as the music requires. Stiff shoes tend to make the dancing very heavy and unattractive.

PENDULUM – FORWARD AND BACK BASIC MOVEMENTS

This is a forward and back movement and it can be used with a slight lean back on a forward step and a slight lean forward on a backward step. The lean is typical of the original character of the dance. Steps should be small, at no time encroaching on the partner's foot placement and, where the instruction is 'pressure but without weight' the foot closes, pressing into the floor and then that same foot is used again.

STARTING POSITION

Commence facing partner in normal hold, Man with weight on right foot, Lady with weight on left foot.

STEP 1

Count: 2 beats – slow

Man: Left foot forward, leading Lady to step back onto her right foot.

Lady: Right foot back.

STEP 2

Count: 2 beats – slow

Man: Right foot closes to left foot, with pressure but without weight change, leading Lady to close her left foot to her right foot.

Lady: Left foot closes to right foot, with pressure but without weight change.

STEP 3

Count: 2 beats – slow

Man: Right foot back, leading Lady forward onto her left foot.

Lady: Left foot forward.

STEP 4

Count: 2 beats – slow

Man: Left foot closes to right foot, with pressure but without weight change, leading Lady to close her right foot to her left foot.

Lady: Right foot closes to left foot, with pressure but without weight change.

LEFT TURN OR SAMBA ROLL

This is a turn to the left, with very small steps and it creates a rolling effect. The man leans slightly forward on the first three steps and slightly backwards on the second three with the reverse for the Lady. Six steps complete the actual figure, but the roll can be repeated as many times as required.

STEP 1
Count: ¼ of a beat – slow
Man: Left foot forward, commence to turn to left, leading Lady back onto her right foot.
Lady: Right foot back, commence to turn.

STEP 2
Count: ¼ of a beat – 'a'
Man: Right foot to the side and slightly back, continue to turn to the left, leading Lady to the side (small step).

Lady: Left foot to the side, small step, and continue to turn.

STEP 3
Count: 1 beat – slow
Man: Left foot crosses in front of right foot, leading Lady to close her right foot to her left foot.
Lady: Right foot closes to left foot.

STEP 4

Count: ¾ of a beat – slow

Man: Right foot back and continue to turn to the left, leading Lady forward onto her left foot.

Lady: Left foot forward and continue to turn to the left.

STEP 5

Count: ¼ of a beat – 'a'

Man: Left foot to the side (small step), leading Lady to the side onto her right foot (small step).

Lady: Right foot to the side (small step).

STEP 6

Count: 1 beat – slow

Man: Right foot closes to left foot, leading Lady to cross her left foot in front of her right.

Lady: Left foot crosses in front of right foot.

ADVANCED WHISK – TO THE LEFT

This is a figure introducing three steps to two beats of the music. The steps are very small and the 'a' count, where the foot crosses behind, is on the ball of the foot only. Here, the knee action is of major importance and the step can be danced as many times as required.

STARTING POSITION

Commence facing your partner in normal hold, Man with weight on right foot, Lady with weight on left foot.

STEP 1
Count: ¾ of a beat – slow
Man: Left foot to the side, leading Lady to step to the side onto her right foot.
Lady: Right foot to side.

STEP 2
Count: ¼ of a beat – 'a'
Man: Right foot behind left foot, toe to heel, leading Lady to place her left foot behind her right foot.
Lady: Left foot behind right foot, toe to heel.

STEP 3
Count: 1 beat – slow
Man: Replace weight into left foot, leading Lady to replace weight into her right foot.
Lady: Replace weight into right foot.

ADVANCED WHISK – TO THE RIGHT

STEP 1

Count: ¾ of a beat – slow

Man: Right foot to the side, leading Lady to step to the side onto her left foot.

Lady: Left foot to the side.

STEP 2

Count: ¼ of a beat – 'a'

Man: Left foot behind right foot, toe to heel, leading Lady to place her right foot behind her left foot.

Lady: Right foot behind left foot, toe to heel.

STEP 3

Count: 1 beat – slow

Man: Replace weight into right foot, in place, leading Lady to replace weight into her left foot.

Lady: Replace weight into left foot, in place.

LADY'S UNDERARM TURN TO RIGHT

The Lady's Underarm Turn to the left or to the right is a very popular figure. Here, the Man dances his Whisk in place, raising his arm to lead the Lady to turn to her right or to her left. His arm must be raised sufficiently high for the Lady to turn under it without having to duck her head and giving her comfortable space to turn. The fingers from both parts of the partnership should be soft and relaxed, and while the Lady is turning under the arm there is no strong hold. Her fingers just turn within the palm of the Man's hand.

STARTING POSITION

Commence facing partner in normal position, Man with weight on the right foot, Lady with weight on the left foot.◁

STEP 1

Count: ¾ of a beat – slow
Man: Left foot to the side, leading Lady to take a small step forward commencing to turn to the right.
Lady: Small step forward to the right, turning to the right under raised arms.

STEP 2

Count: ¼ of a beat – 'a'
Man: Right toe behind left foot, leading Lady to take a small step to the left to turn to the right under raised arms.
Lady: Small step to the left, turning to the right under raised arms.

STEP 3

Count: 1 beat – slow
Man: Replace weight into left foot, leading Lady to complete her turn to the right and to end in normal position.
Lady: Small step to the right turning to the right under raised arms to end facing partner in normal position, having made a small circle under arm.

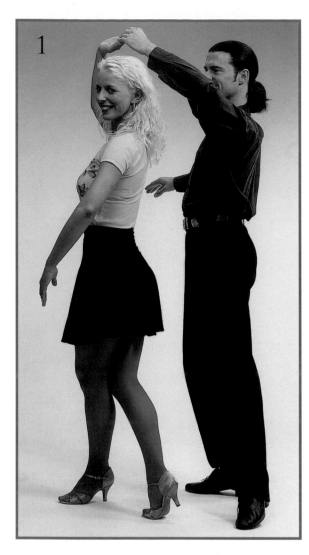

LADY'S UNDERARM TURN TO LEFT

STEP 1
Count: ¾ of a beat – slow

Man: Right foot to the side, leading Lady to take a small step forward commencing to turn to the left.

Lady: Left foot forward, small step, turning to the left under raised arms.

STEP 2
Count: ¼ of a beat – 'a'

Man: Left toe behind right foot, leading lady to step forward on her right foot commencing to turn to the left under raised arms.

Lady: Right foot forward, small step, turning to the left under raised arms.

STEP 3
Count: 1 beat – slow

Man: Replace weight into right foot, leading Lady to take a small step forward onto her left foot, turning under raised arms and to end in normal position.

Lady: Left foot forward, small step, turning to the left under raised arms to end facing partner in normal position.

SPECIAL TIPS

★ Stand naturally upright with no tension in the shoulders or arms. For the Man, try to understand the leads so that the Lady can comfortably dance the figure or steps required of her. Listen to the music carefully before starting to dance, and use the four-bar introduction to exercise the knees to the rhythm before actually dancing the steps. Be confident that you are reacting to the correct musical beat. Do not hold the Lady too tightly with the right hand. It is there just to guide, not to hold the Lady towards the Man. The left hand should be kept naturally on the Man's own side or the Lady's right hand on her own side, joined together in a relaxed fashion.

★ **The Samba Roll** This roll is almost like a beer barrel rolling forward or backward. When stepping forward the body will roll slightly forward. △

★ **The Samba Roll Backwards**

This roll is made by stepping back so that the body will roll slightly backwards. Slightly is the key word. Because there are two people dancing together do not overdo it unless you are a very well trained dancer. Just employ a very slight roll action of the body forward and the body backward, leaning from the waist only and making the waist as free and mobile as possible. It is fun and it gives the original character to the step. △

★ **SUGGESTED CHOREOGRAPHY**

The Pendulum Step, when going forward, leaning slightly back and when going back, leaning slightly forward, gives the effect of the pendulum. Very gently, very slightly and the emphasis is on slightly. This figure could become very uncomfortable and you could suffer loss of balance if the movements were too exaggerated.

Suggested Choreography

1.	Side Basic x 4	4 bars
2.	Side Cross x 4	4 bars
3.	Promenade Walks x 4	4 bars
4.	Carnival Walks x 4	4 bars
5.	Advanced Whisks x 4	4 bars
6.	Left Foot Pendulum and turn to left x 8	8 bars
7.	Left turn or Samba Roll x 4	4 bars
Repeat from side Basic		32 bars total

THE TANGO

$\mathcal{T}$HE TANGO IS A DANCE which has its own language and it appeals to nearly all those who wish to learn dancing. Its history goes back hundreds of years and in the land of its origin it is almost a religion.

The social Tango is quite easy to learn because it is based on normal walking. There is no rise and fall and all the steps are quite flat-footed. For the Man they are mainly walking forward and for the Lady they are mostly walking backwards. However, in the Promenade position, the Lady will walk forward. There are, of course movements which require the

use of the ball of the foot, such as the second step of turns. It is the interpretation of the music and its relation to the step which will produce the staccato action required to give this dance its character – rather quicker 'quicks' and slower 'slows'. But this can only be achieved by constant practice and awareness of how the steps relate to the music, and to the shape of the figure being danced, whether it is a Forward Walk or a Promenade position, so popular in the Tango.

The music has a very clear, danceable beat. However, some Tango music sounds quite classical and finding the beat for dancing can be difficult. The strong staccato beat in the music will encourage the dancer to make strong shapes such as the 'check' or 'contra check'. For these movements the Lady will feel an exaggerated lead from the Man which helps her to make the head and body shape. Always wear pliable shoes and rehearse a soft knee action. Study the difference in the hold of the Tango. It is very different to the Waltz, Foxtrot and Quickstep, because the Man's right arm is a little further around his partner than in the other dances and the Lady's left hand is placed below the Man's shoulder, not on top of the arm as in the other dances. As her body position is also slightly different, study these aspects of the dance before attempting to lead your partner.

A final thought, perhaps that will help you to achieve the true character of the dance, is to think of yourself making footprints in the sand with each step.

TANGO WALKS

These are a series of two walks: left foot, right foot and curving to the left.

STARTING POSITION

Commence in Tango position with Man's weight on right foot, Lady's weight on left foot.

STEP 1

Count: 2 beats – slow
Man: Left foot forward, leading Lady back onto her right foot.
Lady: Right foot back.

STEP 2

Count: 2 beats – slow
Man: Right foot forward, leading Lady back onto her left foot.
Lady: Left foot back.

LEFT TURN – LADY OUTSIDE PARTNER

STARTING POSITION

Commence facing towards centre, Man's weight on right foot, Lady's weight on left foot.

STEP 1

Count: 1 beat – quick

Man: Left foot forward, commencing to turn left, leading Lady back onto her right foot.

Lady: Right foot back.

STEP 2

Count: 1 beat – quick

Man: Right foot to side and slightly back, continue to turn left, leading Lady to the side, onto her left foot.

Lady: Left foot moves slightly to the side.

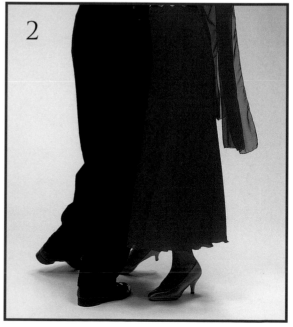

STEP 3 *Count: 2 beats – slow*
Man: Left foot back, partner outside, leading Lady forward onto her right foot.
Lady: Right foot forward, outside partner.

STEP 4 *Count: 1 beat – quick*
Man: Right foot back, turning to left, leading Lady forward onto her left foot, now in line with partner.
Lady: Left foot forward in line with partner.

STEP 5 *Count: 1 beat – quick*
Man: Left foot sideways, continuing to turn left to face outside wall, leading Lady to the side on her right foot.
Lady: Right foot sideways, commence to face partner in normal position.

STEP 6 *Count: 2 beats – slow*
Man: Right foot closes to left foot, completing turn and now *facing* towards the outside of the room, leading Lady to close her left foot to her right foot.
Lady: Left foot closes to right foot, now in normal position with partner.

TANGO CHECK FORWARD AND TAP
STARTING POSITION

Commence facing towards wall with Man's weight on the right foot, lady with weight on the left foot.

STEP 1

Count: 2 beats – slow

Man: Left foot forward with '*check*' action, leading Lady back onto her right foot.

Lady: Right foot back with '*check*' action and making '*head*' shape.

STEP 2

Count: 1 beat – quick

Man: Replace weight back into right foot in place, leading Lady to replace weight forward into left foot.

Lady: Replace weight forward into left foot.

STEP 3

TAP Count: 1 beat – quick

Man: Left foot to the side, small step, in Promenade position, without weight, leading Lady to the side onto her right foot, without weight. ('Tap' action.)

Lady: Right foot to the side in Promenade position, small step without weight. ('Tap' action.)

STEP 4 Promenade

Count: 2 beats – slow

Man: Left foot to the side in Promenade position, leading Lady to the side onto her right foot in Promenade position.

Lady: Right foot to the side in Promenade position.

STEP 5

Count: 1 beat – quick

Man: Right foot forward in Promenade position, leading Lady forward onto her left foot in promenade position.

Lady: Left foot forward in promenade position.

STEP 6

Count: 1 beat – quick

Man: Left foot to the side, leading Lady to the side onto her right foot and commence to turn her to face her partner.

Lady: Right foot to the side turning to face partner in normal position.

STEP 7

Count: 2 beats – slow

Man: Right foot closes to left foot leading Lady to close left foot to right foot and return to normal position.

Lady: Left foot closes to right foot, return to face partner in normal position.

SPECIAL TIPS

★ Tango Hold
The hold of the Tango is slightly different from the hold for the other dances. Here, the right hand is placed slightly further round the Lady's waist and she is very slightly on the Man's right side. ◁ ▽

★ The Check
The Check is a very gentle movement in its social form but it can be developed into an exaggerated Contra-check, which you will see danced by expert Tango or competition dancers. The steps are the same, but the timing can be different. More time can be spent in order to get greater effect. ▽

★ Tango Feet
Because of the walking action and the 'no rise' in the Tango, it naturally curves to the left. You will find that the walks and the left turn will come quite naturally if the hold is correct. The closer hold, with the Lady on the Man's right side, together with the walking action and no rise, will curve the dance to the left. △

THE CHA CHA CHA

HE CHA CHA CHA has evolved from a number of different dances – the Mambo, the Merengue, Street Dance, Disco and Rumba. It is almost a party dance because it has more variations than other dances. The Cha Cha Cha is happy and lively and should not have too many figures. Because of the chassé action, the basic movement should be practised time and time again before adding any variations. Once you have mastered this, then the variations will become easier.

On paper the Cha Cha Cha Chassé to the left and to the right looks easy, but in actual fact the movements require a lot of practice in order to achieve the speed necessary to keep up with the music and the continuity of movement. This is perhaps one of the most difficult aspects of the dance. The music is continuously playing at the same tempo so the dancers must retain that tempo in the feet, lightly, naturally and with speed, small steps and with rhythm so that they match the music.

Always take care to obtain music that is written as a Cha Cha Cha and ensure that the music is not too fast. In the Cha Cha Cha there are four beats to a bar. Each step takes one beat each and then the Cha Cha Cha absorbs the other two. There is no set rule as to whether you start with a Cha Cha Cha Chassé, begin with your left foot in place or commence the dance by going forward on your left foot. It

is entirely up to the dancer to rehearse and then find the most comfortable way to interpret the music. Experts are able to play with the music and to split beats. As a social dancer you do not need to take this on board, but it is a good idea to think of the step as 'Quick, Quick, Quick and Quick'. In other words 'One Two Cha Cha Cha, One Two Cha Cha Cha'. Having achieved this, if you continue to study to a higher level then you will develop the ability to play with the music.

Footwork, as in nearly all Latin dancing, is ball flat or ball of the foot. Quicker steps are on the ball of the foot and strong beat steps are on the ball flat. It is not wise to use a heel lead.

Good poise will help the speed of the dance. The head should be held high. Maintain a good balance, have strong legs and positive foot action.

The couple should stand a little apart with the Man's right hand placed just under the Lady's left shoulder blade, on no account pulling her forward towards him. If anything, the Man should allow the Lady to rest slightly back into the palm of his hand. The hand must be lightly placed and used only as a guide. Remember that when stepping backwards, lower into the back heel later than when you step forward in the dance. This is essential for good poise. If the heel is lowered immediately when the foot steps back then the weight will drop backwards. If it is lowered gently the weight will remain central.

SOLO SPOT TURN (LADY TO RIGHT)
STARTING POSITION

Commence facing partner in 'Solo' position, Man with weight on left foot Lady with weight on right foot.

STEP 1
Count: 2 – quick
Man: Right foot forward turning to left.
Lady: Left foot forward turning to right.

STEP 2
Count: 3 – quick
Man: Left foot forward turning to left.
Lady: Right foot forward turning to right.

Note: The pictures show Man turning to his left and Lady turning to her right.

STEPS 3, 4 & 5

Count: 4 and 1 – quick and quick

Man: Right foot Cha Cha Cha Chassé (right, left, right) to complete whole turn to face partner in normal left 'Solo' position.

Lady: Left foot Cha Cha Cha Chassé (left, right, left) to complete whole turn to face partner in normal or 'Solo' position.

SOLO SPOT TURN (LADY TO LEFT)
STARTING POSITION

Commence facing partner in 'Solo' position, Man's weight on right foot. Lady's weight on left foot. Lady will turn to her left.

STEP 1

Count: 2 – quick

Man: Left foot forward turning to right.

Lady: Right foot forward turning to left.

STEP 2

Count: 3 – quick

Man: Right foot forward turning to right.

Lady: Left foot forward turning to left.

During spot turns, while the Man is turning to his right, the Lady is turning to her left.

STEPS 3, 4 & 5

Count: 4 and 1 – quick and quick

Man: Left foot: Cha Cha Cha Chassé (left, right, left) to complete a whole turn to face partner in normal or 'Solo' position.

Lady: Right foot Cha Cha Cha Chassé (right, left, right) to complete whole turn to face partner in normal or 'Solo' position.

LADY'S UNDER-ARM TURN TO RIGHT
STARTING POSITION

Commence facing partner in normal position, Man's weight on right foot, Lady's weight on left foot.

STEP 1

Count: 2 – quick

Man: Left foot forward, leading Lady to step back onto her right foot.

Lady: Right foot back.

STEP 2

Count: 3 – quick

Man: Replace weight into right foot, leading Lady to replace into her left foot.

Lady: Replace weight into left foot.

STEPS 3, 4 & 5

Count: 4 and 1 quick and quick

Man: Cha Cha Cha Chassé in place (left, right, left), leading Lady to Chassé (right, left, right) raising left arm to prepare Lady for her turn.

Lady: Cha Cha Cha Chassé (right, left, right) raising right arm, preparing for underarm turn.

76

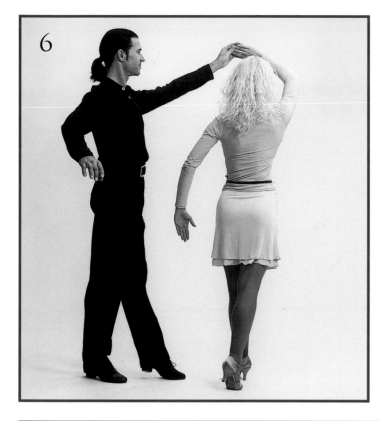

STEP 6

Count: 2 – quick

Man: Right foot back, leading Lady to step forward onto left foot to turn to the right under raised arms.

Lady: Left foot forward turning to right under raised arms.

STEP 7

Count: 3 – quick

Man: Replace weight into left foot, leading Lady forward on right foot to continue to turn to the right.

Lady: Right foot forward turning under raised arms.

STEPS 8, 9 & 10
Count: 4 and 1 – quick and quick
Man: Cha Cha Cha Chassé in place (right, left, right), leading Lady to complete her turn to the right and returning to normal position.
Lady: Cha Cha Cha Chassé (left, right, left) to complete underarm turn and end facing partner.

CHA CHA CHA: HAND TO HAND TO LEFT
STARTING POSITION
Commence in facing position with double hand hold, Man with weight on right foot, Lady with weight on left foot.

STEP 1
Count: 2 – quick

Man: Left foot back turning to left to end in Side-by-Side position, releasing hold with left hand and leading Lady back onto her right foot.

Lady: Right foot back to end in Side-by-Side position, releasing hold with right hand.

STEP 2
Count: 3 – quick

Man: Replace weight into right foot leading Lady to replace weight into her left foot.

Lady: Replace weight into left foot.

STEPS 3, 4 & 5

Count: 4 and 1 – quick and quick

Man: Left foot to side to Chassé (left, right, left) to face partner and take double hand hold, leading Lady to step to the side onto her right foot (right, left, right).

Lady: Right foot to the side to Chassé (right, left, right) to face partner in double hand hold.

CHA CHA CHA: HAND TO HAND TO RIGHT

STEP 1

Count: 2 – quick

Man: Right foot back, turning to right to end in Side-by-Side position, releasing hold with right hand, leading Lady to step back onto her left foot.

Lady: Left foot back to end in Side-by-Side position releasing hold with left hand.

STEP 2

Count: 3 – quick

Man: Replace weight into left foot, leading Lady to replace weight into her right foot.

Lady: Replace weight into right foot.

STEPS 3, 4 & 5

Count: 4 and 1 – quick and quick

Man: Right foot to side to Chassé (right, left, right) to end facing partner, leading Lady to step to the side onto her left foot to end in double hand hold.

Lady: Left foot to the side to Chassé (left, right, left) to end facing partner in double hand hold.

SPECIAL TIPS

★ The Cha Cha Cha is a Latin dance and therefore non-progressive. It is danced almost entirely In-place. Practise the Cha Cha Cha Chassé to the left, and to the right many times. Add the two strong steps which divide the Chassés. Try to keep the legs under the body and the steps only the width of the hips. Stepping outside the width of the hips will create bad balance. It is inevitable when learning that your steps will be too big to begin with, so when practising, try all the time to reduce the size of the steps and keep them well under the body.

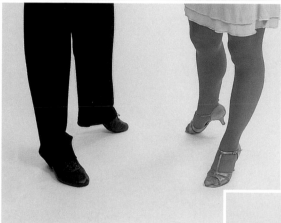

★ Solo spot turns △
These are turns on the spot, turning solo, using individual interpretation and they can be repeated as many times as required. It is essential to remember that having turned, the Cha Cha Cha Chassé then completes the turn. Without it the turn will be out of time with the music. Each turn is one complete turn to either right or left.

★ Direction around the ballroom
The Cha Cha Cha does not have any direction around the ballroom. Steps can be taken in any direction and should be small, compact and with regard to the number of people on the floor and the size of the floor.

★ Hand Hold
Hands should be held lightly. The Man's palm faces upwards and the Lady's palm faces downwards. ▷

★ Underarm Hold
Hold the hands lightly. Do not grip them. The Lady turns under her raised arm so ensure that her arm is held high enough to avoid her having to duck underneath. ▽

THE QUICKSTEP

*T*HE QUICKSTEP is perhaps one of the most popular dances in a dance programme, or even in a sequence programme, because so many attractive Quicksteps have been produced as sequence dances. This is probably due to its light, easy, lilting rhythm. The feeling of go, go, go when you listen to the music, and the fact that the steps are small and rhythmic and, if selected properly, relate to the music.

The Quickstep here is in three sections and these three parts should be amalgamated to dance as one unit.

It is important to listen carefully to the music and to tap out the beats with the foot to get accustomed to the speed and the gliding feeling that the dance produces. Some Quickstep music has a polka-type effect. It is not advisable to use this music unless you are a very experienced dancer. Choose music with a more smooth and rhythmic approach.

The Quickstep has been influenced by many dance crazes, including the Charleston, and a Charleston feeling can be felt in the music of many Quicksteps. Therefore the dancer will add steps because of that Charleston feeling, by twisting the feet. Often the Quickstep has been described as 'The Trickstep' because of the tricky little foot movements that can be included, once you are in control of the basic steps, with a feeling of flight to music.

The Quickstep is perhaps one of the most played dances at any social dance and therefore it is essential that you study this as one of the priority dances. Tempos can vary from fast to medium, to slightly slow, depending on the type of tunes and the interpretation of the music. The Quickstep is a dance which is used worldwide and whatever country it is played in, it does not change its character.

QUARTER TURN TO THE RIGHT

STARTING POSITION:

Commence facing towards the wall, weight on Man's left foot, Lady's weight on her right foot.

STEP 1

Count: 2 beats – slow

Man: Right foot forward commencing to turn slightly to the right, leading Lady to step back onto her left foot.

Lady: Left foot back.

STEP 2

Count: 1 beat – quick

Man: Left foot to the side continuing to turn very slightly to the right, leading Lady to step to the side onto her right foot.

Lady: Step to the side onto right foot.

STEP 3

Count: 1 beat – quick

Man: Right foot closes to left foot, leading Lady to close her left foot to her right foot.

Lady: Left foot closes to right foot.

STEP 4

Count: 2 beats – slow

Man: Left foot to side and slightly back, no further turn, leading Lady to step to the side and slightly forward onto her right foot.

Lady: Right foot to the side and slightly forward.

QUICKSTEP CHASSÉ

STEP 5
Count: 2 beats – slow
Man: Right foot back with slight turn to the left, leading Lady to step forward onto her left foot.
Lady: Left foot forward.

STEP 6
Count: 1 beat – quick
Man: Left foot to side with a slight turn to the left, leading Lady to step to the side onto her right foot.
Lady: Right foot to the side.

STEP 7
Count: 1 beat – quick
Man: Right foot closes to left foot, leading Lady to close her left foot to her right foot.
Lady: Left foot now closes to right foot.

STEP 8

Count: 2 beats – slow

Man: Left foot to the side and *very* slightly forward, leading Lady to step to the side onto her right foot.

Lady: Right foot to the side.

STEP 9

Count: 2 beats – slow

Man: Right foot forward, outside partner on her right side, leading Lady to step back onto her left foot.

Lady: Step back onto left foot, to end with partner on the outside.

FORWARD LOCK STEP

STEP 10
Count: 1 beat – quick
Man: Left foot forward, leading Lady to step back onto her right foot.
Lady: Right foot back.

STEP 11
Count: 1 beat – quick
Man: Right foot crosses behind the left foot on the balls of both feet, leading Lady to cross left foot in front of right foot.
Lady: Left foot crosses in front of right foot on the balls of both feet.

STEP 12
Count: 2 beats – slow
Man: Left foot forward and slightly to the side on ball of foot, leading Lady to step back onto her right foot.
Lady: Right foot back.

RIGHT TURN
STEP 13
Count: 2 beats – slow

Man: Right foot forward, outside partner on her right side, leading Lady to step back onto her left foot and commence to turn to the right.

Lady: Left foot back and commence to turn to right.

STEP 14
Count: 1 beat – quick

Man: Left foot to side, continue to turn to the right, leading Lady to step to the side onto her right foot.

Lady: Right foot to the side.

STEP 15
Count: 1 beat – quick

Man: Right foot closes to the left foot, completing the first part of the turn, leading Lady to close her left foot to her right foot.

Lady: Left foot closes to right.

STEP 16

Count: 2 beats – slow

Man: Left foot back (*small step*), leading Lady to step forward onto her right foot and commence turn to the right, quite strongly.

Lady: Right foot forward, strong turn to the right.

STEP 17

Count: 2 beats – slow

Man: Right foot to the side (*small step*), continue to turn to the right, leading Lady to step to the side onto her left foot.

Lady: Left foot to the side and then continue turning.

STEP 18

Count: 2 beats – slow

Man: Left foot forward, continuing to turn to the right. End facing the wall, leading the Lady to step back onto her right foot. End backing towards the wall.

Lady: Right foot back to end backing towards wall.

SPECIAL TIPS

★ Because of the speed of this dance always check the comfort and width of your dancing shoes because feet need freedom to expand as they are dancing and should not be held tight.

★ The Lock Step

The Lock Step needs to be practised continuously. Place weight onto the left foot and toe and at the same time, put strong pressure into the ball of the foot. Cross your right foot behind with a transfer of weight.

Repeat 'step and cross, step and cross, step and cross' until you feel the ankles crossing, the strength in the ball of the foot, and the ankle power that you need to maintain balance when dancing a Lock Step. The Lady should practise travelling backwards, going back on the right foot, on the ball of the foot, and not letting the heel touch the floor and crossing the left foot in front. Then repeat 'back cross, back cross, back cross' many times to get the feeling of actually dancing a Lock Step with balance, small steps and precision. When you introduce it into the dance, you will only have to dance one set to feel comfortable and easy. ▷

Correct Lock Step

Incorrect Lock Step

★ The Hold

The hold is a close hold, but not so close that either partner is pulled off their own feet. At all times, the dancer should be standing upright on their own feet and not encroaching on the space of their partner. This particularly applies to the top part of the body as it is so easy for the Man to pull the top of the Lady towards him with his right hand – or the Lady to pull the top of the Man towards her with her left hand. This will put the partnership out of balance and it would become very cumbersome and even out of control over a period of time during a dance.

★ The Ankle Rise

This needs practice for both Man and Lady to achieve the good balance needed for the speed of the dance. △

THE MERENGUE

*T*HE MERENGUE is the national dance of the Dominican Republic and various neighbouring islands. It is very popular throughout the Caribbean and South America and through chart hits, it has become very popular throughout Europe.

Merengue music is very varied and mastering the dance is a question of listening to and understanding the beats because the tempos also vary a great deal and are not always consistent. The Merengue can go from a slow beat, to a medium, to a very fast tempo, and that is the challenge of the dance. The dance itself was never really designed as a 'couple' dance. It really has much more of a Carnival and party atmosphere. In Europe the Merengue has been developed as a 'couple dance', and delightfully so, because the couple can make up their own choreography. They can dance a few figures in hold, then a few 'solo' doing exactly what they feel, without relating to their partner at all.

The dance has huge challenges and it is great fun at a party. Many of the chart tunes, as well as pop video music of the day, can be used for Merengue. It is in two-four time, with two beats to a bar of music and each step takes one beat. The footwork is, as in all Latin dances, on the ball of the foot. Strong pressure into the floor is needed, through the ball of the foot. All the figures are danced, from the basic movement, forward and back or Chassé sideways, and then dancing into the various patterns. The ideal way to learn is to practise the basic 'in place' and the basic side steps, the basic forward and back, gradually developing the choreography with a partner or as a solo dance, using the arms to make shapes above the head or down by the side. Even some disco shapes go extremely well to Merengue music. It is a dance to enjoy.

THE MERENGUE

The Merengue is a very easy foot pattern. It consists of a continuous 'marking time' action, i.e *Right. Left. Right. Left or Left. Right. Left. Right. Left. Right.*

While 'marking time' with your feet and matching this to the music, march forwards, backwards and Chassé sideways to the left and right, walking in a circle shape.

Convert the marching steps and marking time steps to some of the shapes and patterns shown on these pages, or make up your own choreography, with underarm turns, leading the Lady around your back, oversways and splits.

There are many exciting shapes and patterns to make. This dance is so popular because it has no real discipline. Sometimes you can dance with a partner and sometimes solo.

The Merengue originated in some of the hotter countries of the world, where carnivals are so much part of the culture and a great deal of the dance takes place in the open air.

Many chart numbers can be used for Merengue, especially those in two/four timing. Try it: you will love the freedom, the chance to improvise and the opportunity to be your own choreographer.

These are some of the exciting patterns, steps and shapes you could use to make your dancing interesting.

These shapes and patterns can be achieved with careful rehearsal.

SPECIAL TIPS

★ This dance has no set technique but all the steps should be small and extremely rhythmic.

★ Create your own patterns and choreography, at the same time enjoying the freedom of the dance.

★ Listen to the music and feel the phrases of intense rhythm. Use 'marking time' or soft 'marching' steps in time to the beat of the music.

THE JIVE

THE JIVE HAS BEEN DEVELOPED from many forms of dance. With this dance, the challenge is not to have set patterns, but to listen to the phrasing of the music, and to feel that your steps fit the music and that you are free to do the changing shape as the music dictates. Once you have mastered the basic Chassé In-place, the Link and the Fallaway, you are then set up to dance all the other patterns, provided that you keep the Basic Link step and the two Chassés consistent. It is not necessary in a normal Social Jive to alter the step pattern. As it remains consistently 'One two, Chassé left, Chassé right' and then 'one two' of the linking step again, taking you into whatever pattern you decide to do. When

practising the Jive Start with the Chassé. Continue to practise the Chassé to the left and to the right, until you have become very mobile. You should be dancing on the balls of your feet, with your knees relaxed and nice and flexible, but not bent. Practise until the movements feel very natural. Then add the Link step, which is a 'one two, back on the left, replace on the right', or in the case of the Lady: 'back on the right, replace on the left'. You will find that the set pattern of 'one two, back on the left, replace on the right' really is the whole dance. This pattern changes shape slightly throughout the dance. If you are facing your partner, you will step straight back, but if you are in a hold with your partner, the same pattern of 'back replace' can become the Fallaway. Practise the change of places from right to left beforehand.

In the Jive there are many times where the arm is lifted to make an archway. (In some versions of the Jive, this arm movement may be called a 'Loop' or a 'Turn'.) Practise arm shapes so that you get used to raising your arm. The Man should get used to raising his own arm, allowing the Lady to go under her own arm, and the Lady must also practise her own shape so that she lifts her own arm and does not duck her head when wanting to go under the arm.

All the variations shown in the pictures and described will work out if you keep that basic step pattern. Even the 'Chicken Walks' work out as a 'one two, one two three four', so that it maintains some of the basic timing.

JIVE CHASSÉS TO LEFT AND RIGHT (MAN OR LADY)

CHASSÉ TO LEFT STARTING POSITION:
Commence by facing your partner in a double-hand practice hold.

STEP 1

Count: 1 – ¾ of a beat
Man: Left foot to the
side (small step).
Lady: Right foot to side.

STEP 2

Count: 'a' – ¼ beat
Man: Right foot closes
towards left foot.
Lady: Left foot half
closes to right foot.

STEP 3

Count: 2 – 1 beat
Man: Left foot to the
side (small step).
Lady: Right foot to the
side (small step).

CHASSÉ TO RIGHT

STEP 1

Count: 1 – ¾ beat

Man: Right foot to the side (small step).

Lady: Left foot to the side.

STEP 2

Count: 'a' – ¼ beat

Man: Left foot closes towards right foot.

Lady: Right foot closes towards left foot.

STEP 3

Count: 2 – 1 beat

Man: Right foot to the side (small step).

Lady: Left foot to the side (small step).

BASIC LINK AND FALLAWAY

STEP 1
Count: 1 – 1 beat
Man: Left foot back.
Lady: Right foot back.

STEP 2
Count: 2 – 1 beat
Man: Replace weight forward into right foot.
Lady: Replace weight forward into left foot.

Continue with Jive Chassés to left. (left, right, left)

Note: The double hand hold indicates a closer hold.

LINKING STEPS
STEP 1
Count: 1 – 1 beat
Man: Left foot back.
Lady: Right foot back.

STEP 2
Count: 2 – 1 beat
Man: Replace weight into right foot.
Lady: Replace weight into left foot.

Note: The one hand hold indicates an open hold.

STEP 3
Count: 3 – ¾ beat
Man: Left foot forward.
Lady: Right foot forward.

STEP 4
Count: 'a' – ¼ beat
Man: Right foot almost closes to the left foot.
Lady: Left foot closes to the right foot.

STEP 5
Count: 4 – 1 beat
Man: Left foot forward – small step – returning to normal position.
Lady: Right foot forward – small step – returning to normal position.

SIDE BY SIDE 'BUMP'

This movement is danced side by side using Chassés to the left and to the right, and the Basic Link.
Count: 3 & 4, 3 & 4, 1, 2

HAND CHANGE VARIATIONS

CHANGE HANDS BEHIND BACK

This is danced using Chassés to the left and to the right, travelling forward and passing on the Man's left side. The Basic Link is used to return to a facing position, changing hands as your partner is passing by.

CHICKEN WALKS FROM OPEN POSITION

The Chicken Walk is danced by the Lady using walks forward and by the Man, using walks back.

UNDERARM TURNS

The Lady turns under the arm of the Man towards both the left and right.

AMERICAN SPIN
The Lady spins strongly to her right on her right foot, completing a whole turn to the right, to finish with a Chassé (left, right, left).

SPECIAL TIPS

★ One of the most important elements of the Jive is to exercise the knee and leg muscles as this dance works mainly below the knees using a continuous 'down into the floor' action. Jive music is rather slower than Rock/Jive, with slightly different foot patterns.

★ Hand Communication
This is of great importance because use of the hands is the only way that either partner can communicate the direction and steps of the dance with the other.

★ Double Hand Hold
Hold the hands lightly with the Man's palms facing upwards and the Lady's palm facing downwards. ▽

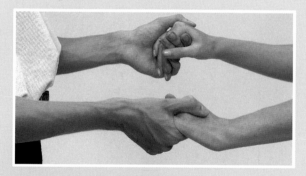

★ Hand Change: Right to Right
The Man uses his right hand to take the Lady's right, dropping their left hands. ▽

★ Hand Change Behind Back
As you turn away from each other, the hands pass across the back and change position.▽

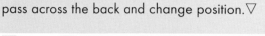
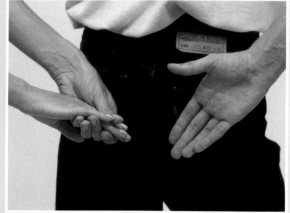

★ Fallaway Position
Both dancers turn out from each other and face forward in a Promenade position. ▽

113

THE RUMBA

THE RUMBA is known for its beautiful melodies and its choreography should show that it is the dance of Love. In its social form, the steps are small and rhythmic, relying on a steady rotary movement of the hips with soft knee flexing. This basic action comes from the Rumba's country of origin. When the women carry wood bundles on their heads they walk flat-footed, with a hip swing, absolutely upright and head erect, in order not to drop what they are carrying.

This foot and body action is typical of the way the dance should be performed. There are many forms of the Rumba. Bolero, Mambo and even the Cha Cha Cha are derivations of Rumba, and usually the type of music being played will indicate that it is a Rumba rhythm. A tune such as *Spanish Eyes* would suggest a very slow, sensuous dance, but *Tea for Two* or *Wheels Cha Cha* would immediately tell you that the faster beat means a Cha Cha Cha. The Rumba is a very popular cabaret dance and can be choreographed with ballet figures to make it romantic and to add excitement.

The social dancer only requires four or five figures. Usually only one or two Rumbas will be played during an evening dance, a wedding or a cruise, but these figures should be well-rehearsed.

The music is written in four-four time, which means it has four beats to a bar of music. Each beat should be given its full value because the dance is using three steps to four beats of music, which makes one of those steps last a little longer. The general feeling would be: Quick – one beat, Quick – one beat, Slow – two beats. There are many interpretations of this timing but for the elementary dancer, quick, quick, slow is sufficient and efficient.

The Rumba hold must be relaxed, with the dancers standing a little apart. The Man's right hand should be just under the left shoulder blade of the Lady, not holding tight, but guiding her. His left arm is rounded and the Lady's right hand is in his left hand with a very relaxed action.

When a step is made the body should always be balanced – upright but not stiff. The full weight is taken onto the moving foot and the stance is maintained, taking care not to throw the head and shoulders forward, as this will cause your partner to lose their balance.

The Rumba does not have a set alignment, in relation to the Ballroom. It mostly turns to the left – if it turns at all – and the 'apart' or 'solo' movements can be danced on any alignment because it is generally considered a static dance.

This dance requires a flat-footed action and strong legs to motivate hip action.

SPOT TURNS TO RIGHT AND LEFT

These turns have an individual feeling. They should be as their title suggests: on the spot, small steps and turning in a very small circle.

STARTING POSITION

Commence facing your partner in 'Solo' Position. Man's weight on right foot, Lady with weight on left foot.

TO THE RIGHT
STEP 1
Count: 1 beat – quick
Man: Left foot forward, commence his turn towards right.
Lady: Right foot forward, commence her turn towards the left.

STEP 2
Count: 1 beat – quick
Man: Right foot forward, continue to turn to the right.
Lady: Left foot forward, continue to turn to the left.

STEP 3
Count: 2 beats – slow
Man: Left foot to the side to end facing partner having made one complete turn to right almost in place, walking round an imaginary small circle.
Lady: Right foot to side to end facing partner.

TO THE LEFT

STEP 1

Count: 1 beat – quick

Man: Right foot forward, commence to turn to the left.

Lady: Left foot forward, commence turn to the right.

STEP 2

Count: 1 beat – quick

Man: Left foot forward, continue turn to the left.

Lady: Right foot forward, continue turn to right.

STEP 3

Count: 2 beats – slow

Man: Right foot to the side to end facing partner. Complete one whole turn to the left almost in place, walking round an imaginary small circle.

Lady: Left foot to side to end facing partner.

LADY'S UNDER-ARM TURN (TO HER RIGHT)

The Man dances his basic movements in place, making sure he raises his left arm and the Lady's right arm high enough for her to turn under without ducking her head and to be able to move her right hand very softly and comfortably within the Man's left hand. A tight hold in these two hands will make it very difficult for the Lady to turn.

STARTING POSITION

Commence facing partner in normal hold, Man's weight on right foot, Lady's weight on left foot.

STEP 1
Count: 1 beat – quick
Man: Left foot forward.
Lady: Right foot back.

STEP 2
Count: 1 beat – quick
Man: Replace weight into right foot.
Lady: Replace weight into left foot.

STEP 3
Count: 2 beats – slow
Man: Left foot to the side – small step.
Commence raising joined hands.
Lady: Right foot to the side – small step, raising right arm and preparing for a turn to the right.

STEP 4

Count: 1 beat – quick

Man: Right foot back, leading Lady to step forward on her left foot to commence a turn to her right under raised arms.

Lady: Left foot forward turning to right under raised arms.

STEP 5

Count: 1 beat – quick

Man: Replace weight into left foot, leading Lady forward on her right foot to continue to turn under raised arms.

Lady: Right foot forward, continuing to turn to right under raised arms.

STEP 6

Count: 2 beats – slow

Man: Right foot almost closes to left foot, leading Lady to complete her underarm turn to the right, completing a small circle to her right.

Lady: Left foot forward, completing the underarm turn to the right and ending facing her partner in normal position.

LEFT FOOT SHOULDER-TO-SHOULDER

This, as the title suggests, is where the man turns his left shoulder towards the lady, and she turns her left shoulder towards him, and that left shoulder passes slightly outside the lady's left side.

STARTING POSITION

Commence facing partner, Man at a slight angle to her left side with weight on right foot, Lady's weight on left foot.

STEP 1

Count: 1 beat – quick

Man: Left foot forward to end on the outside of partner on her left side, with a double hand hold, leading Lady to step back onto her right foot.

Lady: Right foot back to end with partner on the left side in 'Shoulder-to-Shoulder' position.

STEP 2

Count: 1 beat – quick

Man: Replace weight into right foot, leading Lady to replace weight into her left foot, still in 'Shoulder-to-Shoulder' position and double hand hold.

Lady: Replace weight into left foot, still in 'Shoulder-to-Shoulder' position and double hand hold.

STEP 3

Count: 2 beats – slow

Man: Left foot to the side to end facing partner in a double hand hold, leading Lady to step to the side onto her right foot with a slight turn to the left.

Lady: Right foot to the side to end facing partner in a double hand hold with a slight turn to the left.

RIGHT FOOT SHOULDER-TO-SHOULDER

STEP 1

Count: 1 beat – quick

Man: Right foot forward to end on the outside of partner on her right side, with a double hand hold or Solo position, leading Lady to step back onto her left foot.

Lady: Left foot back to end with your partner on your right side in 'Shoulder-to-Shoulder' position.

STEP 2

Count: 1 beat – quick

Man: Replace weight into left foot, leading Lady to replace weight into her right foot, still in 'Shoulder-to-Shoulder' position.

Lady: Replace weight into right foot, still in 'Shoulder-to-Shoulder' position.

STEP 3

Count: 2 beats – slow

Man: Right foot to the side to end facing partner in normal hold, leading Lady to step to the side onto her left foot.

Lady: Left foot to the side to end facing partner in normal hold.

SPECIAL TIPS

★ The Rumba requires flexible hips, small steps and good poise. Work on shoulders and expressive hands.

★ **Underarm Turn**
Make sure that, when turning the Lady, the hands are only held lightly and not gripped too tight as this will inhibit the turn.

Note for the Lady: Always hold your head high when turning under raised arms. ▷

★ **Shoulder-to-Shoulder**
Although called the 'Shoulder-to-Shoulder', when dancing, the shoulders do not actually touch.
The action is towards the shoulders and the foot goes towards the Lady, left side or right side, and the shoulder turns towards, but does not actually touch. With this figure, there are many other little foot actions, like flicking the foot, that can be developed when the basic pattern is mastered. ◁ ▷

GLOSSARY OF TERMS

ad lib: Repeat the steps or figures as required.

Alignment: The position of your feet in relation to the room.

Beat: The note of the music used for the step. Sometimes two beats are used for one step, in which case the music is said to have a slow beat; sometimes one beat is used for one step, in which case it is known as having a quick beat.

Chassé: This is a sideways movement where the feet close then open.

Choreography: The composition or arrangement of a dance. In social dancing the steps of three or four figures in each dance are all that is really necessary. A dance loaded with variations often proves to be anti-social in a crowd and an unnecessary burden on the dancer.

Close Hold: The two bodies are close together. This is the normal hold for most ballroom dances.

Competition dancing: This is an extravagant style of dance, specially choreographed and specially dressed. It is designed for couples who wish to have their standard of dancing assessed by adjudicators.

Direction: This mostly applies to Ballroom dances which are described as the 'moving' dances and must have correct directions around the ballroom or club.

Fallaway: A position where both partners step backwards to cross behind and automatically open out.

Following: The role of the Lady is to follow the Man. Learning to follow and be led is as much a part of the art of dancing as learning the steps. The Lady must develop a sensitivity to the Man's lead and at no time attempt to take on the role of leader.

In-place: This instruction indicates that you should not travel backwards, forwards or sideways. It is also described as marking time.

Leading: The Man leads the partnership. Leading requires an understanding of every step and change of step for each dance. He must be able to transmit his intentions to his partner and he must also understand the music in order to indicate on which beat of the music to start each dance.

Musical count: The time taken for each step when dancing to music. A slow count is when a step takes two beats and a quick count is when a step takes one beat. (See **Beat**.) As in the Cha Cha Cha the actual words 'Cha Cha Cha' are used in the musical count.

Open Hold: A hold in which the two bodies are slightly apart, as in most Latin dances.

Practice Hold: The hold with which to practise steps at first before taking a Close or Open Hold. It is known as the double hand hold.

Preparation step: The step that precedes a new movement. It is also a term used for the starting foot, before starting to dance any step.

Promenade: Both the Lady and Man are facing in the *same* direction and will dance in that direction, in contrast to normal dance position where they face each other.

Side-by-side: A dance position in which both dancers are facing the same way ready to dance in that direction.

Social: The type of dances used for social occasions such as weddings, holidays or a party. They should be simple, in smart style and the dancer should use small steps and keep awareness of other dancers.

Whisk: This is a movement where one foot crosses behind the other foot.

WHY JOIN A DANCING SCHOOL?

You will learn all the basic steps required to make you proficient by using this book at home. It is a convenient way in which to overcome any natural shyness about being 'left-footed' in public. There is, however, much to be said for also joining your local dancing school, especially if you want to advance and improve your technique.

A good dancing school should be able to teach you how to dance, giving encouragement and confidence, as well as providing social events in which you can participate. Many people want to dance as a way to meet people of all ages who have a similar interest. Dancing schools are not just for those who want to become competitive dancers.

Some areas have more than one school to choose from, so talk to your friends and visit them to see for yourself which one you think is most suitable for your requirements. Here are some of the things to look out for and some of the questions you should ask.

Where is it?
A dance school needs to be convenient either to your home or place of work. Make sure that there are car parking facilities, or it is close to public transport. Will you be safe at night?

Do the school hours suit you?
Is the school open at times convenient to you and offering the classes you want at these times? Do they have facilities for children if required?

What fees are payable?
Many schools have a membership fee, which gives you access to all facilities. Some will offer a price for a series of classes or private lessons Check if these need to be paid for in advance or if they can be paid for in instalments.
Does the school feel comfortable?

When looking around a school, consider whether you would feel welcome and comfortable being there. Ask about social functions such as Tea Dances and Social Dance evenings.

Are the classes crowded?
Check out how many people are usually in a general class. Also, ask what facilities are available for individual classes.

What are the classes like?
A good school will offer a variety of classes for all levels, ages and abilities.

What are the general facilities like?
It is a good idea to look at the changing rooms – are they clean and tidy with a good standard of hygiene? Are the reception areas clean and welcoming with friendly staff?

What are the refreshment areas like?
There should be clean, comfortable bar or refreshment areas where it is pleasant to meet new and old friends. The food on offer should be fresh and healthy.

You will now be able to put into practice all the steps you have learnt from this book.

To find your nearest dancing school, look in the Yellow Pages, or contact the British Dance Council. (See Useful Contacts & Information.)

USEFUL CONTACTS & INFORMATION

ALL DANCE INFORMATION
British Dance Council
Terpsichore House
240 Merton Road
South Wimbledon
London SW19 1EQ. UK
Tel: + 44[0]20 8545 0085
Website: british-dance-council.org

Ballroom Dancers Federation
Administrative Office
8 Hazelwood Road
Cudham
Sevenoaks
Kent TN14 7QU. UK
Tel: + 44 [0]1689 855 143
Website: bdfi.org

World Rock 'n' Roll Confederation
Wolfgang Steuer
Schutzenstrasse 8
D-80335 Munchan. Germany
Tel: + 49 89 59 67 05
Website: wrrc.org
The above will be able to give advice on dance classes and general dance information

DANCE ACCESSORIES
Dance Sport International Ltd
Unit 4
The Courtyard
Aurelia Road
Croydon CR0 3BF. UK
Website: dancesport-international.com
DanceSport sell dance shoes for both competition and social dancing, accessories, and have a large range of dance videos, dance music cassettes, CDs and books.

DANCE SHOES
Supadance Shoes
Supadance International
159 Queens Road
Buckhurst Hill
Essex IG9 5BA. UK
Tel: + 44[0]20 8505 8888

Julienne
163 High Street
Beckenham, Kent. UK
Tel: + 44[0]20 8650 5796

Freed of London
94 St Martins Lane
London WC2N 4AT. UK
Tel: + 44[0]20 7240 0432
Website: freedoflondon.com
The above shoe manufactures specialize in most types of dance shoes.

CLOTHES
Chrisanne
14 Locks Lane
Mitcham
Surrey CR4 2JX. UK
Website: chrisanne.co.uk
Boutique Tel: + 44 [0]181 770 1827

Choice London Ltd
Old Book House
324-44 London Road
Mitcham
Surrey. UK
Tel: + 44 [0]181 715 9200

Faberge Fabrique Ltd
2a St. Helen's Road
Norbury
London SW16 4LB. UK
Tel: + 44 [0] 181 679 6547
Website: dance-shop.com

MUSIC
Ross Mitchell
1 Queen's Road
Fleet
Hampshire GU13 9LA. UK
Tel: + 44 [0]1252 629 740
Website: danceandlisten.com

Tema International
151 Nork Way
Banstead
Surrey SM7 1PB. UK
Tel: + 44 [0]1737 219 607
Website: termadance.com

WRD
282 Camden Road
London NW1 9AB. UK
Tel: + 44 [0]171 267 6762/3/4

C&D Dance Records
145 Chestnut Avenue
Eastleigh
Hants. SO50 5BB. UK
Tel: + 44 [0]1703 614476
Website: freewebs.com/candddance
Also see DanceSport International Ltd.

Peggy Spencer's easy-to-follow dance instructions are also available on video for both *Absolute Beginners* and those ready for *The Next Steps*. They are available from all good video stockists priced £10.99

TURNING POINTS IN HISTORY

Revised and Updated

The Irish Famine

The Birth of Irish America

H www.heinemann.co.uk/library
Visit our website to find out more information about **Heinemann Library** books.

To order:
☎ Phone 44 (0) 1865 888112
🖺 Send a fax to 44 (0) 1865 314091
💻 Visit the Heinemann Bookshop at www.heinemann.co.uk/library to browse our catalogue and order online.

First published in Great Britain by
Heinemann Library,
Halley Court, Jordan Hill, Oxford OX2 8EJ,
part of Harcourt Education.
Heinemann is a registered trademark of
Harcourt Education Ltd.

Editorial: Clare Lewis
Designed by Tokay Interactive Ltd.
(www.tokay.co.uk)
Printed in China by WKT Ltd

10 digit ISBN: 0 431 07712 6
13 digit ISBN: 978 0 431 07712 3
10 09 08 07 06
10 9 8 7 6 5 4 3 2 1

**British Library Cataloguing in
Publication Data**
Allan, Tony
Turning Points in History: The Irish famine:
The Birth of Irish America – 2nd edition
941.5'081
A full catalogue record for this book is
available from the British Library.

Acknowledgements
The Publishers would like to thank the
following for permission to reproduce
photographs:
Corbis, p **28** (Ed Kashi); pp. **24**, **29** (Jan
Butchofsky); Hulton Getty, pp. **4**, **9**, **19**, **21**,
22 , **27**; Illustrated London News,
p. **5**; Mary Evans Picture Library, pp. **6**, **7**, **8**,
10, **12**, **13**, **14**, **16** (and top front cover),
17, **20**, **23**, **25**, **26**; The Art Archive, pp. **11**,
15.

Cover photograph reproduced with
permission of Bridgemann Art Library/
© Trustees of the Watts Gallery, Compton,
Surrey, UK.

The publishers would like to thank Stewart
Ross for his help in the preparation of this
book.

Every effort has been made to contact
copyright holders of any material reproduced
in this book. Any omissions will be rectified
in subsequent printings if notice is given to
the Publisher.

The paper used to print this book comes
from sustainable resources.

Contents

Some words are shown in bold, **like this**. You can find out what they mean by looking in the Glossary.

The great hunger

A family tragedy

"On Sunday last, 20 December, a young woman begging in the streets of Cork collapsed and was at first unable to move or speak. After being given 'restorations' and taken home to her cabin, she told those helping her that both her mother and father had died in the last fortnight. At the same time she directed their attention to a heap of dirty straw that lay in the corner and apparently concealed some object under it. On removing the covering of straw, the spectators were horrified to behold the corpses of two grown boys. . . There they had remained for perhaps a week and maybe a fortnight."

So wrote a government inspector sent to investigate conditions in western Ireland in December 1846, at the height of the Irish famine. In its horrific details, his report told of the individual tragedies that lay behind a national calamity. In the small town of Skibbereen alone, he found that 169 people had starved to death in just three weeks. In nearby Goleen, so many people were dying that local people had rigged up a coffin with a sliding base to use for repeated burials.

In the winter of 1846, the small town of Skibbereen in southwest Ireland saw some of the worst horrors of the Irish Famine. Government inspectors estimated that about 200 people died of hunger in the town in the months of November and December alone.

The greatest disaster

The famine was, quite simply, the greatest disaster ever to afflict Ireland, and it was all caused by a plant disease. Potato was the staple food of the Irish poor, and when potato **blight** laid waste to the harvest for several years in a row the consequences were catastrophic. In just five years it killed one million people and turned a country with a rapidly expanding population into one that declined for a century.

It also drove even larger numbers abroad. Unable to make a living at home, Irish men and women travelled in their tens of thousands to mainland Britain and to Canada, often voyaging in overcrowded ships and risking disease. But most found their way to the United States, where in the ports of Boston and New York, they laid the foundations of what would one day be a thriving, nationwide Irish-American community.

These pictures from the *Illustrated London News* of August 1846 show a healthy potato plant with a picture showing signs of the potato disease *(Phytophthora infestans)*, which caused the Irish famine.

No lack of food?

One of the oddest facts about the famine was that food continued to be exported from Ireland throughout the years of hunger. Even in Skibbereen when hundreds were dying, a local inspector reported that "On Saturday, notwithstanding all this distress, there was a market plentifully supplied with meat, bread, fish, in short everything." The problem was not so much a lack of food as the extreme poverty of the poorer people, who had no money to buy the supplies that were available.

Rulers and rebels

A troubled land

Although unmatched in its horror, the famine was just one in a series of tragedies that had dotted Ireland's history. The island had known a time of greatness in the troubled centuries after the collapse of the Roman Empire (5th to 9th centuries AD), when its monks and artists helped keep the flame of European civilization alight. Politically, however, it was split between warring kingdoms, and the divisions were to prove its undoing.

The English connection

In 1171, King Henry II of England took advantage of Irish feuding to claim overlordship of the island, and from that time on Ireland's destiny was inextricably linked with that of England. Unlike Scotland and Wales, which also once fought with England and yet came to live peaceably with their bigger neighbour, Ireland never willingly accepted the relationship.

One problem was sheer distance; Ireland was cut off from London by the Irish Sea, and lawmakers in the British capital rarely had Irish interests uppermost in their minds. Language was another problem, for until the early 19th century most Irish people spoke **Gaelic** rather than English. An even bigger stumbling block was added with the religious upheavals of the 16th century, when England adopted the **Protestant** faith while Ireland remained true to Roman **Catholicism**.

England's Protestant King William III leads his men against a Catholic Irish army at the Battle of the Boyne in 1690. William's victory set the scene for the "Protestant Ascendancy", a period of more than a century during which Irish Catholics saw many of their civil rights taken away.

Divided loyalties

At a time when most wars involved religion in some way, this split had serious implications. In foreign affairs, Catholic Ireland's sympathy lay with other Catholic countries, who were often England's enemies.

To solve this problem, Queen Elizabeth I began encouraging English and Scottish Protestants to settle in Ireland by giving them grants of land. These Protestant settlements caused bitterness, and helped stir up a series of armed revolts that were put down with much bloodshed. A particularly significant uprising in support of James II, deposed as king of England for his tyrannical and Catholic leanings, was crushed by his Protestant successor, William of Orange, at the Battle of the Boyne. The conflict divides the Irish to this day; many Northern Irish Protestants still call themselves Orangemen to honour William's cause.

A rather fanciful portrayal of a peasant rebels' camp at Vinegar Hill in County Wexford during an uprising against British rule in 1798. It was quickly put down by government troops, but in the course of the revolt, a dozen captured Protestants were put to death (shown on the left).

The Act of Union

The final stage in Ireland's subjugation followed another unsuccessful uprising in 1798. By the Act of Union of 1801, Ireland lost her own parliament and became subject to direct rule from London as part of the United Kingdom of Great Britain and Ireland.

After the Act, calm seemingly settled on Ireland, but appearances were deceptive. Under the surface, tensions simmered. Ireland was a divided society. People were divided over many issues, including religion, language, and wealth.

The two Irelands

The humiliation of the penal laws

After the Catholic defeat at the Battle of the Boyne, Ireland's religious divisions were written into law. The victorious Protestants forced through a series of measures collectively known as the **penal laws**. These made it illegal for any Catholic to hold office, stand for Parliament, vote, join the armed forces, or go to university. Worse still, Catholics were not allowed to buy land. Those who already owned it had to subdivide their estates on the death of the head of the family between all the surviving children – unless any converted to Protestantism, in which case they got the lot.

The Protestant Ascendancy

The result of these measures was that by the late 18th century, Catholics, who made up the bulk of the population, owned less than 5 per cent of Ireland's land. All the rest belonged to Protestants, who often lived in magnificent style – their wealth can still be seen in the splendid mansions they constructed across the Irish countryside and in their elegant town houses in Dublin.

A mansion in County Wicklow suggests the grand manner in which the wealthy landowners of the Protestant Ascendancy lived. The Ascendancy also spawned a dazzling culture, graced by writers such as Jonathan Swift, author of *Gulliver's Travels*, and the playwright Richard Brinsley Sheridan.

Scraping by

For the rest of the population, though, the situation was very different. Although a few wealthy landowning families survived, most Catholics had to scrape along as best they could. Many rented land from Protestant landlords, who tended to see them not as tenants to whom they had responsibilities, as in England, but simply as sources of income. Feeling ill at ease amid Gaelic-speakers, few big landowners chose to spend much time on their estates, preferring to lead comfortable lives in Dublin or London instead.

The penal laws created a society in which discontent could not be openly expressed. The Catholic peasantry, for the most part, learned to put up with their lot; the only alternative was occasional outbursts of violence, usually put down with great severity by the soldiers who maintained the established order.

A mother in the town of Clonakilty, near Skibbereen, begs for money to buy a coffin to bury her dead baby.

Peasant rebels

With no political voice to speak for them, Irish peasants joined secret societies to protect their interests. A Frenchman who toured Ireland in 1796 described such groups at work: "They assembled at night in great numbers in certain parts of Ireland, and in order that they might recognize each other safely, they wore their shirts outside their clothes, from whence came the name of 'White Boys'. In this garb they overran the country, breaking the doors and gates of [their targets'] houses, and if they could catch the [landowners'] cattle they mutilated them by cutting off their tails and ears. All the time they did no other violent act, and a traveller might have gone through the country with perfect security."

9

The scourge of poverty

Poverty and the penal laws

The most obvious effect of the social system that developed out of the penal laws was that much of the population lived in grinding poverty. There were corners of prosperity, notably in Ulster, which was inhabited largely by Protestant settlers from Scotland who could make their voices heard. There, a flourishing linen industry developed in the late 18th century.

Workers prepare linen at a textile mill in County Down in 1783. There was little industrial production in Ireland before the famine, and what there was became concentrated in the northeastern province of Ulster.

An underdeveloped land

For the most part, though, industrialization was something Ireland knew little about. It did not have the coal and iron that fuelled the manufacturing revolution then under way in mainland Britain, and the social system in Ireland did little to encourage the people to improve things. The countryside remained underdeveloped; by 1848, there were about 8,000 kilometres (5,000 miles) of railway in Britain as a whole, but only 600 kilometres (375 miles) in Ireland.

For the Catholic majority scraping a living off the land, conditions were often appalling. Those who owned their own farms worked ever-smaller holdings as the land was continually subdivided. Yet they were better off than most of the population, who were forced to rent small plots, often on one-year **conacre** leases that meant they could be **evicted** almost at the landlord's whim. Even so, because of the demand for land in a country with few other jobs, rents were ruinously high – almost double those in England.

Living on the edge

Over much of Ireland, furniture was a luxury few could afford. A survey of the village of Tullaghobegly in County Donegal in 1837 revealed that its 9,000 inhabitants had between them just 10 beds, 93 chairs, and 243 stools. Most people slept and ate on the beaten-earth floors of their hovels.

Life on the bottom

The result was the lowest standard of living in Europe. The 1841 **census** revealed that nearly half of all families in the countryside were living in single-room mud cabins without windows; in parts of western Ireland, the proportion was three-fifths. Yet even these **hovels** were not the bottom of the heap; tenants who were evicted or labourers without land were reduced to putting roofs over ditches or living in holes burrowed out of earth banks. The Duke of Wellington, one-time prime minister of Britain as well as an Irish landowner himself, knew what he was talking about when he told the House of Lords in 1838 that, "There never was a country in which poverty existed to the extent it exists in Ireland."

A farmer's wife serves a meal in a poor cabin. Furniture was a luxury for most Irish people at the time.

11

The potato to the rescue

The potato feeds a nation

In the terrible social conditions of the early 19th century, much of Ireland survived on a single crop – the potato. Originally introduced by Protestant settlers, it had spread across the nation in the 18th century, partly because it was useful in breaking up the land for sowing grain.

A healthy diet

Soon, though, it won popularity in its own right. It was easy to grow and was highly productive – half a hectare of land planted with potatoes, could feed a family of six, where grain would have required five times as much land. The potato was also nutritious. A potato diet, balanced by some dairy produce, salt, and cabbage, provided wholesome sustenance for people of all ages. The same visitors who were shocked by the abject poverty of rural Ireland often commented approvingly on the healthy appearance of the peasantry.

The result was that across much of the country people became increasingly dependent on the potato. Typically, women and older children consumed 5 kilograms (11 pounds) – the equivalent of two medium-sized supermarket bags – each day, and working men even more, averaging 6.3 kilograms (14 pounds).

In good times, even poor families could live quite well if, like this one, they had a store of potatoes in the loft and some pigs and poultry to provide meat and eggs to supplement the diet.

Nothing was wasted. Peelings and potatoes too small for cooking were fed to poultry or pigs, which could be fattened and sold to pay the rent. The pig manure went to fertilize the potato fields.

Some regions became more dependent on the potato than others. In the "oatmeal zones" of Ulster and north Leinster, even the poor could usually supplement their diet with oats, but in large parts of south and west Ireland, the potato was the only significant food.

The risks of dependence

People were aware at the time of the dangers of over-dependence on a single crop. For all their benefits, potatoes did not keep well, and could not be stored from one season to the next. There had even been crop failures in the past, but they had generally been localized and short lived. In general the potato had proved less liable to bad harvests than cereal crops.

Mostly, though, there was simply no alternative to the potato, and so the nation's reliance on it grew. By 1845, an estimated 1.5 million **landless** labourers and their families depended on it almost entirely, and for another 3 million it was the main food. If people did think of an Ireland without potatoes, they quickly put the thought from their mind – the prospect was just too terrible to dwell on.

The failure of the potato harvest was most likely to threaten the survival of the poor. This peasant and his daughter, whose home is little more than a hovel, would be the first to suffer from such a calamity.

More mouths to feed

An exploding population

The situation in the 1840s was made more dangerous because Ireland had experienced a population explosion over the previous 100 years. In 1741 there had been fewer than 2.5 million Irish, but by 1800 the figure had doubled, and it continued to rise. The 1841 census recorded more than 8 million people, and even that was thought to be an underestimate. Britain's future prime minister, Benjamin Disraeli declared Ireland to be the most densely populated country in the whole of Europe.

Farm labourers who had made the trip to England to help with the harvest queue for places on the boat back to Ireland. Seasonal work overseas helped ease the burden of unemployment at home.

The hungry millions

At first sight it seems odd that the population should have risen in the face of intense poverty, but in fact the two factors went together, much as they still do in the world's poorest countries today. It was actually among the landless peasants that the rate of growth was highest. While Irish farmers tended to wait until their thirties before getting married, carefully saving to be able to afford the expense, the very poor had no such worries. For them, no outlay was necessary; a couple could leave their own families' crowded mud cabins and build one of their own for nothing in days. Having no possessions to begin with, they expected none after marriage. Asked by an 1835 commission of enquiry why the poor married so young, a Catholic bishop replied, "They cannot be worse off than they are, and they may help each other."

Support in old age

Typically, poor couples married at 16 or 17, and went on to have large families. They had every reason for doing so – in a society without pensions, children were a couple's only hope of support in old age.

Even so, the growing numbers drained the resources of the country. Some of the surplus children went to swell the population of Dublin, which multiplied four times over between 1700 and 1800. Otherwise, the pressure on the land increased. Areas of mountainside and bog were brought into cultivation and existing agricultural land was further subdivided to provide ever smaller parcels of land for families to live off.

Ultimately, however, all the population growth depended on the availability of a cheap food supply, and that meant the potato. In 1845, this basic staple was suddenly threatened in a totally unexpected way.

The elegance of Sackville Street in the heart of Dublin was a far cry from the city's teeming slums, where most of the population lived. One observer of these reported: "I have frequently surprised from 10 to 16 persons, of all ages and sexes, in a room not 15 feet (4.5 metres) square , stretched on a wad of filthy straw swarming with vermin."

First signs of trouble

The potato blight

The disaster that struck Ireland in the autumn of 1845 was a new disease – the potato **blight**. Its symptoms were black spots on the upper leaves of the plant and a whitish mould underneath. The potatoes themselves often looked wholesome on the outside, but the insides quickly turned to a stinking mush. The blight flourished in mild, damp weather, leading scientists at the time to consider it a form of wet rot. In fact it was a fungus *(Phytophthora infestans)* whose spores were spread by wind and insects, rapidly affecting entire districts.

The blight had first appeared in the United States in 1843, reaching continental Europe in the spring of 1845, probably through shipments of infected seed. At first, Ireland seemed to have been spared; the early crop in August was excellent. But when the late harvest was gathered in October, at least a third of the potatoes were found to be affected.

Discovering the blight

A well-to-do farmer described the experience of discovering the blight when it reached central Ireland: "On August 6, 1846 – I shall not readily forget the day – I rode up as usual to my mountain property, and my feelings may be imagined when before I saw the crop, I smelt the fearful stench . . . [Before long] the luxuriant stalks withered, the leaves decayed, the disease extended to the tubers, and the stench from the rotting of such an immense amount of rich vegetable matter became almost intolerable."

A family struggles to come to terms with the failure of their potato crop. Nobody had any doubts that starvation threatened if the blight turned the potatoes rotten.

A sense of crisis

No one at the time doubted the seriousness of the situation. The government in London, headed by Sir Robert Peel, acted quickly to help. A relief commission was set up in Dublin to co-ordinate the activities of some 650 local committees established to provide famine relief. A system of **public works** was also financed by the government so that work could be given to the unemployed to help with beneficial projects such as road building. An English civil servant named Charles Trevelyan, the head of the Treasury, was given the job of supervising the relief effort from London.

Although never popular in Ireland, the Conservative prime minister Sir Robert Peel in fact took firm action to lessen the first effects of the famine.

Peel also went further, secretly authorizing the purchase of a large quantity of maize from America. He never intended to give this directly to the hungry, instead it was to be kept in government depots and released on to the market if food prices rose too high, so as to prevent **profiteering**. In 1846 Peel repealed the Corn Laws to cut the price of corn, but it still remained too expensive for the Irish poor.

Peel's measures could not prevent suffering in Ireland; there was terrible hunger and an epidemic of typhus fever. Even so, he left office after a general election in 1846 knowing at least that no one had died of starvation alone during his time as prime minister. Worse was to follow in the years to come.

The terrible winter

A time of foreboding

The summer of 1846 was a time of foreboding in Ireland. Even in good times, these were the "hungry months" when one potato crop was exhausted and the next had yet to be harvested. Now there was the fear that, with the country's reserves already exhausted, the new crop would be diseased too.

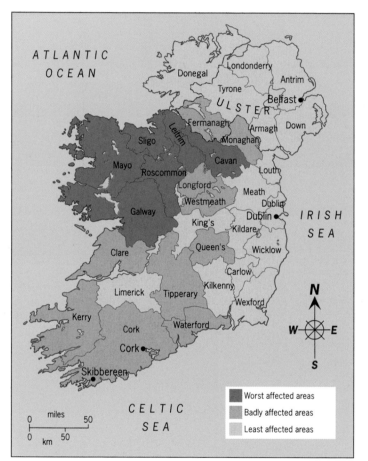

While most of Ireland suffered from the effects of the potato famine, the worst-hit areas were in the west and south of the country.

There was also a fresh government in London, under Lord John Russell. He chose to leave Charles Trevelyan at his post as the famine relief co-ordinator, and that summer Trevelyan made a fateful decision. Fearing above all to increase the burden on British taxpayers, he determined not to buy in extra grain supplies.

The blight returns

In Ireland, people's worst fears were soon realized. A warm, wet summer provided ideal conditions for the blight to spread. By August it was apparent that the crop would be disastrously affected; in fact – nine-tenths were eventually lost.

Only government action on a massive scale could have prevented calamity, but the government did almost nothing. It believed that **market forces** should be left to work, which meant leaving the economy to run as it always had, so even exports of grain from Ireland were not banned. Relief of the starving was left principally to local landowners, even though they had already shown themselves for the most part unwilling to shoulder the burden.

Saving money, not lives

Even when the full scale of the tragedy became apparent, Trevelyan remained more concerned by the need to save money than lives. While admitting in a private letter that "This is a real famine, in which thousands and thousands of people are likely to die," he went on to insist, "If the Irish once find out there are any circumstances in which they can get free government grants, we shall have a system of mendicancy [begging] such as the world never saw."

Famine fever

The result was hunger on a devastating scale, and in its wake came disease. In their weakened condition, famine victims fell prey to horrific and often fatal diseases such as typhus, yellow fever, and dysentery. Shocked eyewitnesses described whole villages where much of the population lay sick and starving on the floors of their cabins, listless with "famine fever".

For those of the **destitute** who could still help themselves, there was only the remnants of Peel's system of public works. There were never enough jobs to go round, even though wages were kept at near-starvation levels so as not to undercut other sources of employment. Worse still, wages were often paid late. As the terrible winter of 1846–47 wore on, reports of deaths of workers on relief schemes became common.

At the height of the famine, a mother and son search despairingly for undiseased potatoes in a field of stubble. Faced with starvation, families would often eat rotten and stinking potatoes that they would not even have fed to their animals normally.

Why was more not done to help?

Aid for the victims

Many millions of people in Ireland, mainland Britain, and further afield were appalled by the famine and did all in their power to help the victims. In Ireland, good landowners waived rents, and provided work for the destitute and food for the hungry. In England, a charity called the British Association raised not far short of £500,000 – worth at least 50 times that in today's money – Queen Victoria herself gave £2,000. Similar amounts were raised in America, where Congress made warships available to transport food; over 100 cargoes arrived in 1847 alone.

The US frigate *Macedonian* docks at Cork in July 1847, bringing food donated in America in response to famine appeals. The US government loaned two naval vessels to carry the supplies to Ireland.

Setting up soup kitchens

In Ireland itself, some of the most effective work was done by the **Quakers**, who set up **soup kitchens** in distressed areas from November 1846. These proved so successful that they finally persuaded the British government into a short-lived change of heart. In January 1847, the relief co-ordinators scrapped the previous system of public works and instead opened soup kitchens of their own, substantially reducing the number of deaths over the summer months. However, the kitchens were considered too expensive to be more than a temporary measure – come the autumn, they were closed, to fatal effect.

An act of God

The fact was that throughout the crisis, only the government could have mobilized the resources needed to avert disaster, and it failed to take sufficient action. There were many reasons why. Tragedies like the famine were regarded at the time as calamities sent by God about which little could be done. There was no tradition of government intervention in the past. When an earlier famine had wiped out a tenth of the Irish population a century before, no action had been taken at all. Many people believed that the deaths, however tragic, were the only possible solution to over-population and poverty in the long run.

Market forces

Most important in the minds of people like Charles Trevelyan, though, were notions of political economy. In their view, markets worked best when left to themselves. They thought that the growing demand for food in Ireland would create new sources of supply, so that any attempt by government to intervene could only do harm. While their ideas might have made sense in a developed economy like England's, they could never have worked in Ireland. There, even in good times, millions of people had no money. In such extreme conditions, notions of a market economy became meaningless.

Workers prepare food for the hungry in a soup kitchen run by the Quakers, a charitably minded religious group. Throughout the famine, privately run relief efforts were more effective than government schemes in bringing help to the needy.

A way out over the seas

The emigration option

As people realized the full horror of what was happening, they sought a way out through **emigration**. There was already a tradition of Irish people travelling to North America – about a million had gone in the 30 years before 1845. In 1846, at the start of the famine, 51,752 people emigrated to the United States. By 1847 this figure had more than doubled, and in 1851 emigration reached a peak, with 221,253 Irish men, women, and children making the sea journey.

Emigrants seeking a better life abroad wait on the dockside at Cork to embark for the United States or Canada. The prospect of the journey was terrifying for people who had often never before travelled more than 50 kilometres (30 miles) from their homes.

Many others who left Ireland never got beyond Britain, where the poorer emigrants went to earn the money for the transatlantic voyage by casual labour – a process known as "step migration". By 1847, the streets of Liverpool, Glasgow, and other cities were full of starving people.

The transatlantic crossing

Of those who did make the crossing, many went to Canada, then a British colony. The reasons were economic – fares were cheap on the Canadian timber ships, which offered passages at low prices to fill their empty holds for the return journey.

Conditions on board were mostly appalling. Passengers were normally expected to take food with them for the journey, but few could now afford that luxury. Hunger, overcrowding, and shortages of water and sanitary facilities turned the ships into breeding grounds for disease. Many thousands of emigrants who set sail died on the voyage.

A cold welcome

An eyewitness who travelled in one of the 1847 "coffin ships" described the scene at Grosse Isle, the Canadian **quarantine** station outside Quebec, when the sick were taken from ship to shore in boats. "Hundreds were literally flung on the beach, left amid the mud and stones to crawl on the dry land as best they could." Even so, most were glad to get to land; the vessel had been moored off the island for a week, without medical help or fresh water.

The final destination of most emigrants was the United States; even many of those who sailed for Canada subsequently sought to cross the border. The American authorities avoided the worst of the shipborne epidemics by demanding higher standards of hygiene on board vessels docking at US ports. By 1848, regulations were tightened in Canada, and the worst of the "ocean plague", as it became known, was over.

Conditions on board the transatlantic "coffin ships" of 1847 were as bad as anything in Ireland itself. Typhoid fever spread in the overcrowded hulks, killing many thousands of those who made the voyage.

The empty land

The human outflow continued though, sometimes financed by landowners eager to clear their lands of unwanted tenants. By 1850, some districts of Ireland were becoming depopulated. Entire families – sometimes even whole villages – had gone in search of better prospects across the seas, thousands of kilometres from the country they still thought of as home.

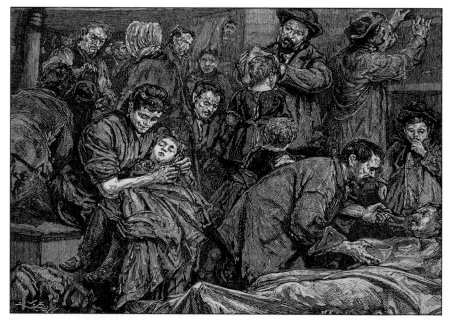

A new life in a new land

The shock of arrival

For the millions who found their way across the Atlantic, life at first was little better than it had been in Ireland. On arrival in Boston and especially New York, they fell victim to fraudsters who regularly cheated new arrivals out of the few possessions they had managed to save.

Even though most **immigrants** came from the countryside, they preferred to stay in the ports where they had first landed to be among other Irish. They ended up living in some of the worst slums in America, often crammed in 10 or more to a room.

Unwanted guests

They also encountered much hostility from their unwilling hosts. Americans had shown great generosity in contributing to relief funds for famine victims in Ireland, but when the poor and starving turned up on their own doorstep, they inevitably saw them as a threat. First and foremost, there were well-founded fears of the diseases they brought with them. It was well known that Montreal in Canada had suffered a typhus epidemic following the first wave of immigration.

Living conditions for many Irish immigrants did not improve in the new country. They often found themselves in the worst slums in America.

A violent underclass

In the early famine years, the cities of Boston and New York, where most immigrants landed, reeled under the impact of the social problems the jobless newcomers caused. In the five years before 1848, the Boston police reported increases of 266 per cent in murders, 1,700 per cent in attempts to kill, and 465 per cent in armed assaults. In addition, 1,500 children below the age of 16 were said to be begging in the streets.

"No Irish need apply"

There were also worries that the low pay for which the unskilled immigrants were prepared to work would undercut US workers' wages. In 1844, even before the famine emigration got under way, there had been anti-Irish riots in Philadelphia that left 13 dead. In fact the first-generation immigrants usually ended up doing the hard, dangerous, and ill-paid jobs that no-one else wanted. Much of 19th-century America's transport infrastructure of roads, railways and canals was the work of Irish hands.

In time, though, the newcomers learned to take advantage of the opportunities offered by the new land. As the Irish-American community took root, it became richer and better respected. Meanwhile, fresh waves of immigrants from other lands took the place the Irish had once occupied at the bottom of the economic ladder.

> Workers lay track for the Union Pacific railway, which eventually linked eastern America with California and the Pacific Ocean. Much of the hard work of building the US railways was done by gangs of Irish labourers.

The ordeal's slow ending

The suffering continues

For those who stayed behind in Ireland, the suffering continued. By 1848 times were hard in mainland Britain too, and the government's over-riding concern was to save money. With the closing of the soup kitchens, the only recourse for the destitute was to seek places in the workhouses. These were prison-like institutions that provided food and shelter in return for unpaid labour. That year saw a surge in the numbers of applicants. Even so, the government in London decided that the extra cost should be borne almost entirely by Ireland alone.

Homeless and helpless

The result was a huge rise in **rates** that ended up **bankrupting** many smaller landowners, who were themselves then forced to join the queues at the workhouse doors. Another effect was to dramatically increase the number of evictions, as landlords sought to get rid of poor tenants whose rates they were expected to pay. In 1850, more than 100,000 people were driven from their homes.

Unable to pay the rent any longer, a family are locked out of their home. Some tenants evicted by landlords ended up dying by the roadsides.

Workhouse life

Sidney Osborne, a clergyman who set out to expose the conditions in Irish workhouses, wrote of one in the town of Limerick: "I have no words with which I can give any real idea of the sad condition of the inmates of two large yards at the parent house, in which were a very large number of young female children; many of them were clothed in the merest dirty rags; they were in the dirt collected on their persons for many weeks; there was not the slightest evidence of the least care being taken of them."

Within the workhouses themselves, conditions were often appalling. Disease was rife, with cholera added to the other epidemics after 1848. In early 1849, as many as 2,500 people were dying each week in the institutions that were supposed to support them.

Starving peasants mob the gates of a workhouse in search of food. However grim and forbidding, these prison-like institutions at least provided meals and shelter, and people fought for places in them.

Counting the cost

There was no clear-cut end to the famine. When its effects did fade from 1850 on, it was mainly because death and emigration had reduced the pressure on resources. The size of the calamity it had wrought was revealed in the national census of 1851. Ireland's population, which would otherwise have been over 9 million, had fallen to 6.6 million. About 1.5 million Irish men and women had been forced to emigrate, the others had died of hunger or disease.

The great debate

The Irish famine virtually destroyed Irish rural society and left a legacy of bitterness that endures to this day. What have been the effects of the famine?

Immediate effects of the famine:

- Approximately one million Irish people died of hunger or disease.
- Approximately 1.5 million Irish people emigrated.
- The overall population of Ireland fell by approximately 2.5 million.
- The British government was hated in Ireland.

Medium-term effects of the famine:

- A large and powerful Irish-American community developed in the United States.
- Many small landowners went bankrupt, their land passing to fewer and fewer large landowners (who often did not live in Ireland).
- Potato growing gave way to sheep and cattle rearing.
- The Gaelic language almost died out.
- The population continued to fall – 4.25 million by 1951.
- Some people mounted increasingly violent campaigns for independence from Britain.
- Tension grew between Protestant Ulster, which was against independence, and the rest of the country, which was Catholic.

Longer-term developments:

- The Irish-American community flourished and some of its members support anti-British movements in Ireland.
- 1921: Ireland was divided between the independent Irish Free State (Republic of Ireland, 1949) and the Province of Ulster (part of the United Kingdom).
- 1968–1998: "The Troubles" in Northern Ireland as Catholics demand fair treatment and union with the Republic.
- The Republic joined the European Community in 1973. The period of spectacular economic growth that followed in the "Celtic Tiger" finally brought the legacy of the famine to an end.

A British soldier patrols the streets of Belfast. This was a common sight during the troubles in Northern Ireland.

Can Britain be blamed for the Irish famine?

Yes!

- England had no right to conquer and govern Ireland in the first place.
- The English looked down on the Irish because they were Catholics.
- Many English landlords saw Ireland just as a source of money.
- British business people failed to build up Irish industry.
- Even when it saw what was happening, the British government refused to spend taxpayers' money to stop the suffering.
- The British government put economic theory above common sense.

No!

- The British government, acting according to what was thought right at the time, believed market forces would sort out the problem.
- The British government had no previous experience of disaster on such a scale – it did not know how to cope.
- Individuals, such as the Prime Minister Sir Robert Peel and Charles Trevelyan, did their best in impossible circumstances.
- The British people as a whole were generous in their donations.
- Famine, like earthquake, is an act of God beyond human control.

What do you think?

Find out more

Using the Internet

Explore the Internet to find out more about the Irish famine. You can use a search engine, such as www.yahooligans.com or www.google.com, and type in keywords or phrases such as *potato blight*, *Irish troubles*, *Battle of the Boyne*, *Irish-America*, or *penal laws*.

More books to read

Barnham, Kay. *Changing Face of Ireland*. (Hodder Wayland, 2005)

Daley, Patrick. *World Tour: Ireland*. (Raintree, 2004)

Timeline

1171		Henry II claims overlordship of Ireland
1534		England breaks with Rome. Henry VIII establishes the Church of England. Ireland remains Roman Catholic.
1584		Elizabeth I seizes land in Munster for English settlement
1610		Large-scale Protestant settlement of Ulster begins
1690		William of Orange defeats Catholics at the Battle of the Boyne
1692		Catholics excluded from Irish parliament. First penal laws passed.
1741		Famine kills one-tenth of Irish population
1798		United Irishmen launch unsuccessful uprising
1801		Act of Union links Britain and Ireland in the United Kingdom
1838		Poor Law establishes network of 130 workhouses across Ireland
1841		Census records Irish population at 8,175,124
1843		Potato blight first appears in the United States
1845	September	First signs of potato blight in Ireland
	November	Charles Trevelyan takes charge of famine relief operations
1846	July	Lord John Russell becomes British prime minister
	November	Quakers set up first soup kitchens
1847	January	British Association forms to raise money for famine victims
	January	Soup Kitchen Act authorizes state-run soup kitchens
	May	First fever cases reach Grosse Isle in Canada
	June	Poor Law Extension Act – Irish ratepayers must meet cost of workhouses
	September	Declaring famine over, government closes soup kitchens
1848		Total failure of potato crop makes famine worse
1849		Queen Victoria visits Ireland
1850		Evictions reach a peak, with 100,000 made homeless
1851		Census shows Irish population has dropped to 6,552,385
1921		Irish Free State established – Ulster remains linked to Britain
1949		Republic of Ireland officially proclaimed
1961		John F. Kennedy, descendant of Irish immigrants, becomes first Catholic president of the United States
1973		Irish Republic joins the European Community

Glossary

bankrupting   causing a state of financial ruin

blight   disease of plants

Catholic   member of the Roman Catholic Church, whose supreme leader is the pope

census   official count of the population

conacre   farmland let for a single season

destitute   without money or the means to make any

emigration   to leave one's own country to live abroad

evict   to turn tenants out of their homes

Fenian   member of any of various 19th-century Irish revolutionary organizations dedicated to ending British rule

Gaelic   native language of the people of Ireland

hovel   poor hut in which people live

immigrants   people arriving in a new country where they wish to settle

landless   owning no land

market forces   relationship between demand for goods and services and their supply. For a government to leave a situation to market forces means they do not intervene because it is felt that demand would automatically lead to a greater supply.

penal laws   laws passed in Ireland in the 17th and 18th centuries to restrict the rights of Catholics

profiteering   taking advantage of a situation to make excessive profits

Protestant   a Christian who is not a member of the Roman Catholic Church

public works   government-financed projects designed to provide jobs for the unemployed

Quaker   member of the Society of Friends, a Christian movement known for its charitable work

quarantine   to place people suspected of having infectious diseases in isolation for a time in order to stop the spread of the disease

rates   a tax based on the value of property

smallholding   piece of agricultural land that is smaller than a farm

soup kitchen   place where free food is provided for the needy

Index